THE PODCAST GUEST PLAYBOOK

TURNING CONVERSATIONS INTO CONNECTIONS AND COMMUNITY

MATTY DALRYMPLE

MARK LESLIE LEFEBVRE

WILLIAM KINGSFIELD PUBLISHERS

Matty and Mark dedicate this book to Michael La Ronn, podcast guest extraordinaire, who has generously shared his insights and knowledge with us and our listeners.

CONTENTS

INTRODUCTION

Welcome to your playbook! If you're here, it means you're considering pitching yourself as a guest on podcasts as a way to get the word out about your work. We believe you've made a great decision.

As evidenced by the hundreds of episodes of Matty's *The Indy Author Podcast* and Mark's *Stark Reflections on Writing and Publishing* podcast, as well as by the numerous podcasts we've guested on, we're obviously big believers in the value of podcasting. Why?

Why Podcasting?

Podcasts serve a growing hunger for information and entertainment that can be consumed on the go. According to Interview Valet's 2026 *State of Podcast Guesting* report, there are over 398K active podcasts (ones that have aired an episode within the previous 30 days).

That popularity is driven by the effectiveness of the medium. Audio enables a connection between speakers and listeners that is difficult to duplicate in written content like articles or blog posts. There's an intimacy to quite literally getting your voice in someone's ear. Listeners get a better sense of you as an individual, and that connection is a vital first step in establishing a *know-relate-trust* relationship, a construct we prefer to the more common *know-like-trust*. The content feels immediate, even if the episode was recorded months or even years earlier. It also feels more personal, even if hundreds or thousands of other listeners are enjoying the same content. And podcast audiences are often highly targeted and deeply engaged, meaning you're speaking directly to people who are genuinely interested in your topic—making it one of the most effective ways to build your brand and expand your reach.

We believe these benefits are especially valuable for authors and other creators, because podcast guesting allows you to showcase your expertise, creativity, and unique voice to reach your audience in a way that the written word simply can't match. It's an opportunity to bring your stories to life, forge a deeper emotional connection with your audience, and share your journey, insights, and passion in an engaging and memorable way. Vitally, in this age of AI, it is—to borrow a phrase from Joanna Penn of The Creative Penn—a chance to double down on your humanity.

Podcast guesting offers these benefits with relatively small investments of time and money. The tech needed for a professional guest presence is relatively inexpensive and generally easy to use, and once you've refined your strategy and tactics, the time needed to land engagements and to execute them effectively will be barely longer than the time you spend chatting with your host. And you can do it all from the comfort of your home studio!

NOTE: In *The Podcast Guest Playbook*, we focus on

authors because that's where our expertise lies, and the writing world provides a wealth of examples to draw from. However, don't put this book down if you aren't an author! The advice we share is designed to help anyone seeking to leverage podcasts as a platform to share their creative work with the world. Whether you're a visual artist promoting your latest exhibit, a musician reaching out to new audiences, an entrepreneur launching an innovative product, or a nonprofit leader championing a cause, the principles and strategies in this book are broadly applicable. While the examples may have a writing-centric spin, the insights can be adapted to fit the unique needs of any creator looking to amplify their voice and connect with an engaged audience.

The Challenge of Guesting

The popularity of the format means that more and more podcasters are stepping up to provide that content, offering you more opportunities to capitalize on these benefits. But that explosion of interest in podcasts, while great for listeners and hosts, creates a challenge for potential guests. Having a huge pool of podcasts to pitch yourself to makes an understanding and prioritization of your goals vital.

Furthermore, the effectiveness of podcasts for building a community means that you'll have many more other potential guests vying for places in those most desirable slots. According to Interview Valet's 2026 *State of Podcast Guesting* report, there are over 100K podcasts seeking guests, but almost 4.8M guests seeking podcasts.

But armed with the advice we share in *The Podcast Guest Playbook*, you'll be well-prepared to pursue those opportunities with confidence and effectiveness. We'll address:

- Planning Your Strategy
- Prepping Your Persona
- Assembling Your Guest Toolkit
- Identifying Your Targets
- Making Your Pitch
- Following Up with Your Host
- Preparing for Your Interview
- Building Rapport
- Delivering Your Interview
- Amplifying Your Appearance

We also explore some other scenarios where podcasting best practices can be applied, such as radio and television interviews.

But before we dive in to an exploration of these best practices, we want to take a look at the three key words in the subtitle of our book: Community, Connections, and Conversation.

Community

By **community**, we mean the relationships you will develop with your podcast listeners. Reaching this audience, and the benefits that can accrue from these relationships, is often the initial impetus for a creator to decide to pursue guest placements. We love how Tom Schwab of Interview Valet frames it in his article "How Nonfiction Authors Can Leverage Podcast Guesting":

Podcast interview marketing allows you to have meaningful conversations with your target audience, in a place they have self-selected to be, and you are being introduced by a trusted source—the podcast host.

This unique aspect of podcasts makes them perfect for a specific kind of audience outreach: content marketing. Content marketing is a strategic marketing approach focused on creating and distributing content that is relevant, consistent, high-quality, and free in order to attract and retain a clearly defined audience, ultimately to drive profitable customer action.

One of the reasons podcast appearances are such an effective form of content marketing is that they are a great way to establish your expertise on your topic. Appearances are also a great résumé-builder for pursuing paid speaking engagements. If Matty wants to pitch an event organizer on a talk about indie publishing short fiction, it's great to have a pool of podcast appearances on that topic to point them to.

This opportunity to create community among a podcast audience is often the initial driver for a creator pursing guest appearances, but there is another aspect of podcast guesting that can yield even greater benefits: the opportunity to form connections with your hosts.

Connections

We believe that the mutual benefits of building a relationship with your hosts is often overlooked and under-leveraged.

Of course, since hosts are the gatekeepers to podcast appearances, it's obvious that guests need to establish some connection with them, but true connections can lead to lifelong relationships and pave the way to other long-term opportunities. We've both built career-long relationships with podcast hosts through appearances on their podcasts.

For example, the relationship we've built that led to us coauthoring this book was based on our frequent appearances on each other's podcast. (Our coauthored book *Taking the Short Tack: Creating Income and Connecting with Readers Using Short Fiction* came about because Matty was a listener of Mark's podcast, showing that these kinds of opportunities can arise from the community of listeners you reach with a podcast in addition to the connections you create with the host.) The book Matty coauthored with M.L. Ronn, *From Page to Platform: How to Succeed as an Author Speaker*, might not have come about had Michael La Ronn not been a frequent guest on her podcast.

Similarly, Mark landed a coauthoring opportunity after one of his many guest appearances on Joanna Penn's long running *The Creative Penn* podcast. Mark and Joanna were talking about the overwhelming stress authors face, and they joked that the two of them should sit around in a comfy lounge wearing smoking jackets and sipping martinis and write a book about helping authors to relax. *The Creative Penn* listeners began commenting and writing in to ask Mark and Joanna to write that book. The book that resulted, *The Relaxed Author*, is an example of a podcast-based connection Joanna has with Mark—one deep enough to consider collaborating on a book—as well as the connection she has forged her listeners, whose passion for the topic fueled the book's creation.

Forging a mutually beneficial professional connection with one host opens the door to invitations from other podcast hosts or even from event organizers. The circle of podcast hosts within a certain niche can be small, and word of a successful guest appearance will spread. Mark considers it one of the greatest honors as a guest when someone hears him on a podcast and is inspired to invite him onto their own show for a similar conversation or to invite him to their event as a speaker.

Mark has not only benefited as a podcast guest but has paid it forward as a podcast host. Since Mark's exposure to an individual through the *Stark Reflections* podcast helps him understand their areas of strength and their professional goals, he has been able to funnel writing and publishing opportunities their way.

And even if your appearance on a podcast doesn't result in the publication of a book, an invitation to provide a keynote address, or even a spike in your book's sales, you still enjoy the experience of speaking with someone who by definition shares your interests, a welcome interlude in the often-solitary life of a creator. Host of the *Turning Writers into Readers* podcast Emma Dhesi says:

I've been interviewing people for a number of years now and it's one of the things I enjoy most about my job. Not only is it a great chance to meet new people but it's a lovely way of staying in contact with people or friends that I've made online who live in another part of the world.

You cement that relationship by thinking of the dynamics of podcast guesting not as "reaching new audiences," which implies a one-sided benefit of you tapping into a host's audience to let them know about your offering, but as "sharing audiences," since you also have a responsibility to share the host's offering—their podcast—with your audience. The mutual benefits and mutual responsibilities between a podcast host and guest is a theme we'll return to throughout this book.

Conversations

And what about the third C in our book's subtitle: conversations?

We recommend you go into every podcast interaction thinking of it less as an interview and more as a conversation. That means showing up with stories, not scripts, and being open to the natural give-and-take that makes for a truly engaging exchange. Above all, never think of it as a sales pitch—doing so is a sure way to distance yourself from your host and your audience.

True conversations are what will make the connections and community possible.

A Fourth C ... and a Caveat

We've discussed the key benefits of podcast guesting: **community** with listeners and **connections** with hosts based on the **conversations** that podcasts enable.

There is another C we should mention—**cash**—and this C comes with a caveat.

Podcast guesting can lead to indirect income, since it's a fantastic form of content marketing, leading listeners to your books, products, or services. However, it's extremely unusual for a guest to earn direct income from a podcast appearance, and those who do are the biggest name celebrities who already have a huge following. But podcast appearances offer significant opportunities for indirect income, by providing a way to acquaint listeners with your offerings. Tapping into that opportunity is a primary focus of this book.

Who Are We?

Matty bases her advice on having hosted hundreds of episodes of *The Indy Author Podcast* and having been a guest on dozens more. She also spent many years in her corporate job facilitating two-day orientation sessions focused on acquainting employees with a set of tools and techniques that would enable them to operate effectively within the company values. A key part of this experience was the stories that the company executives would share with the participants about how those tools and techniques had benefited them professionally and personally. The stories the executives told were key to the success of the sessions, and she was responsible for coaching them to refine their stories. Storytelling is a key component of successful podcast appearances, and we'll share insights on that topic.

Mark draws upon his nearly quarter century of experience with podcasting, first as an enthusiastic listener in the early 2000s, then as the creator and host of three different podcasts as well as a guest on hundreds of podcast episodes and radio and television programs. Mark's first podcast guest appearance as an author was in October 2006 and led to book sales up to a decade later. From 2006 to 2011, Mark hosted his first podcast, *Prelude to a Scream*. From 2013 through 2017, he launched, hosted, and produced the first 100 episodes of Rakuten Kobo's *Kobo Writing Life* podcast. In 2018, he launched his weekly episodes of *Stark Reflections on Writing and Publishing*.

We share our own experiences from both sides of the mic so that you can capitalize on our successes and learn from our slip-ups.

Who Are You?

Who are you? might seem like an odd question to pose in a book, but we hope that among the many ways you define yourself is as an enthusiastic podcast listener, because the best podcast guests are enthusiastic consumers of podcast content.

If you're not already a regular podcast listener, then your first assignment is to become one. Find three podcasts in your topic area and listen to the latest three episodes of each. Pick popular podcasts—probably the ones that will pop up first in a search on your podcast app for your topic area—so you can experience what has resonated most effectively with audiences. Since you won't learn as much about podcast guesting by listening to podcasts that feature a solo host (without a guest), find podcasts that include guests.

Then, for each of these episodes, note one thing you enjoyed about the podcast that would make you want to listen to more episodes and one thing you didn't like that would discourage you from listening. For example, you might enjoy the fact that the podcast host seemed welcoming and interacted in a friendly manner with the guest; you might dislike the fact that the interview was interrupted several times by sponsor promos. This will be valuable fodder for when you're prioritizing the podcasts you want to pitch.

Also note one thing you enjoyed about each guest's performance that you would like to emulate in your own guest appearances and one thing that you didn't enjoy about the guest's performance that you would want to avoid in your own appearances. For example, you might appreciate that the guest reflected some knowledge of their host's background—i.e., they didn't force the conversation to be all about them. You might dislike the fact that the guest's audio quality wasn't good, perhaps the result of using their computer's built-in mic.

If you're struggling to come up with your "likes," or if you found the experience of listening to the podcasts unengaging, you might want to reconsider whether podcast appearances are an opportunity you want to pursue right now. Spend a little more time experimenting with podcast listening, perhaps with ones outside your planned topic area, before beginning to pitch yourself as a guest. If you find yourself drawn to podcasts outside your identified topic area, is there enough overlap that you could shift your focus to those podcasts and tweak your topic appropriately? We'll explore options for this in the "Defining Your Topics" section.

It's vital to be a fan of the medium you want to participate in. After all, you probably wouldn't have become a writer or a sculptor or musician if you didn't enjoy the work of other writers or sculptors or musicians. In the case of podcasts, familiarity breeds comfort and lays the foundation for engaging and productive appearances.

A Few Notes

A few notes about the examples and terminology we use:

- Most of the examples we use are from our experiences in the writing and publishing worlds, but as noted earlier, the advice we share is designed to help anyone seeking to leverage podcasts as a platform to share their creative work with the world.
- We were torn between the use of two terms: "pitch" is the term most people associate with the process of proposing yourself as a guest for a podcast, and although it has a somewhat sales-y connotation— we'd prefer "introduction"—it is easily understandable, so in most cases we stuck with "pitch."
- A similar dilemma arose with "interview." Most people understand this to mean the interaction between you and the host during the recording, but "conversation" much more effectively conveys the tone we recommend those interactions should take. We'll use these terms interchangeably.
- Finally, although it seems awkward, the term "performance" is sometimes unavoidable, despite its

suggestion of being something other than your true self. When we use this term, we intend to convey that you will need to perform to a standard of excellence during your interview, not that you will be enacting a character (although you do want to be enacting the best version of yourself—more on that in the section on "Prepping Your Persona").

For Your Playbook

At the end of each section of *The Podcast Guest Playbook*, we include questions for you to answer; capture your responses in the downloadable document available at theindyauthor.com/playbook. This will encourage you to think through how the information in the book applies to your situation and will improve your chances of acting on it effectively.

For this section, capture notes related to our assignment in this section.

At a strategic level, what are your goals for podcast guesting related to:

- Building community with listeners?
- Building connections with hosts?

At a more tactical level ...

- What three podcasts in your topic area did you choose to listen to?
- For each of three episodes of each podcast ...
  - What was one thing you enjoyed that would make you want to listen to more episodes?
  - What was one thing you didn't like that would discourage you from listening?

- ○ What was one thing you enjoyed about each guest's performance that you would like to emulate in your own guest appearances?
- ○ What was one thing that you didn't enjoy about the guest's performance that you would want to avoid in your own appearances?

UNDERSTANDING THE
HOST PERSPECTIVE

To work effectively with another professional, it helps to understand what their priorities, challenges, and concerns are. As a podcast guest, your pitches and performances will be more effective if you have some understanding of what the priorities, challenges, and concerns are for your hosts. This section will provide you with some behind-the-scenes perspective on podcast hosting. Understanding this helps you work more effectively with them—for example, understanding why a prospective host doesn't reply immediately to your pitch or why a host might not be able to commit to having your interview about your forthcoming book air the day of the book's launch.

To give you a sense of the tasks a host has to juggle to produce a podcast, we've provided below a simplified version of Matty's task list for a single episode of *The Indy Author Podcast*, and this is *after* she has read the pitch, researched the prospective guest, crafted a reply, coordinated the interview scheduling, prepped her materials for the interview, and conducted the interview. You don't need to understand all the details of this list —you just need to recognize that all this is taking place behind the scenes.

- Like / follow guest on social media
- Edit audio and video (reduce word gaps, remove select filler words, insert section titles, look for hook and clips, add graphic header / footer to video)
- Export, edit, and post clips
- Export transcript
- Generate summary and review / edit
- Generate keywords / tags and review / edit
- Script and record intro and outro
- Assemble final audio and video episodes
- Create video thumbnail
- Create social media images
- Draft description text for all platforms (podcast hosting platform, video platform, social media, patron notification, website, etc.)
- Create episode-specific page on TheIndyAuthor.com
- Add episode to main podcast page on website
- Modify video platform customization to reflect latest episode
- Notify guest of availability of episode
- Notify other interested parties of availability of episode
- Schedule episode and clips on social media

Not only is this list long, but for many hosts, the creation of their podcast is a labor of love. They might not receive any money for it, and if they do receive some compensation, it may not even cover their costs.

Podcast hosts spend hours in preparation, execution, production, and promotion to give their guests an opportunity to share their knowledge and highlight their resources.

How can you act on this knowledge?

- Respect the podcaster's time from your initial pitch through your interview and beyond.
- Understand the podcaster's goals and help them to achieve them—for example, by actively promoting not only *your* episode but their backlist episodes as well.
- Treat your host as you would someone who has invited you into their home, recognizing it as a privilege and not a right. Be understanding if a scheduled recording date needs to shift or if your episode isn't promoted on a particular social media platform.

Keeping in mind what's going on behind the scenes will help set your expectations accurately and help you navigate the relationship with your host to your mutual benefit.

For Your Playbook

At the end of each section, we include questions for you to answer—capture your responses in the downloadable document available at theindyauthor.com/playbook. Doing so will encourage you to think through how the information in the book applies to your situation and how you will act on it. For this section ...

- Which if the items in the list of podcast host tasks were the most surprising to you?
- If you're familiar with the podcast production process, what are some other tasks we might have included?

PLANNING YOUR STRATEGY

Now that we've explored the benefits offered by podcast guesting—creating community among listeners and connections with hosts—in this section, we focus on what you need to have in place to make sure your podcast appearances are as effective as possible in terms of supporting your goals. Specifically, we'll look at the three key steps to set up every appearance for success:

Craft copy that grabs the host's attention—in the right way.

Create a reusable pitch template that you can personalize quickly while showcasing the value you'll bring to each show.

Plan your timing so each interview lands when it will serve you, your host, and your audience best.

Crafting Your Copy

We include our advice about crafting the copy early in this section on planning your strategy, because we find that this process helps solidify your ideas about your goals for your podcast appearances and the approach you want to take to pursue them.

Defining Your Topics

The topic of your podcast pitches might seem obvious: the topic of your book or focus of your coaching practice or course or other offering. But as podcast hosts, we are rarely intrigued by potential guests asking if they can come on our podcasts to talk about a product; it sounds promotional and self-serving.

Instead, think of your pitch as focused not on the topic of your offering, but on **topics of conversation related to your offering**.

For example, if we were pitching an appearance to promote *The Podcast Guest Playbook*, the topics we might pitch could include the power of audio content to form strong bonds with listeners; how to craft a winning pitch letter; a checklist to ensure the best audio and video experience for your audience; and how to nurture your relationship with your hosts after the episode airing.

If Mark were pitching an appearance related to his book *Wide for the Win*, the possible topics could include understanding distribution options for ebook, print, and audio; the risks of putting all your eggs in one retailer / distributor basket; the power of making an informed publication / distribution decision about each book; how to avoid common mistakes when publishing wide; and how distribution strategies might change over an author's career.

For Mark's nonfiction books about haunted locations, his topics might be focused on a certain type of building (*Haunted Bookstores / Libraries / Hospitals*) or geographies (*Haunted Ottawa / Montreal / Hamilton / Sudbury*). He could address the psychology behind people's fascination with haunted locations. If his audience was writers, he could discuss the process of research and writing these books, and how authors of such books can pitch publishers.

Fiction authors, too, should strive to focus their pitches on a conversational topic—the story behind the story—not on the book per se. For example, when Matty is looking for opportunities to spread the word about her novel *The Sense of Reckoning*, she can take a historical perspective, describing how she incorporated the events of the Bar Harbor Fire of '47 into the book.

For any book or service you want to promote through podcast appearances, it's useful to have a half dozen such topics you can cover. For a specific podcast, you might choose to pitch these as standalone topics from which a host can choose. Providing a host with several topics gives them flexibility—for example, they may be generally interested in what advice Mark has to share about wide distribution, but their interest might especially be piqued by how an author's distribution strategies might change over their career.

Alternatively, you might combine a few topics into a pitch that you feel will appeal to the host and engage their audience. For example, for a podcast catering to authors earlier in their careers, Mark could propose a conversation that combines a description of distribution options for ebook, print, and audio with a discussion of the risks of putting all your eggs in one retailer / distributor basket.

By focusing your pitches on discussion topics—not the offering itself—you will subtly lead your listeners to your books, products, or services, thereby fulfilling the content marketing potential of podcast appearances.

Drafting Your Description

Once you have your topic list assembled, you can start working on your description. You'll use the information, or variations of it, for:

- Your pitch letter
- Appearance promotion (to be used by both you and your host)
- Other circumstances in which you want to share information on your topic, such as for landing speaking gigs

Start by creating a description of about 100 words and be sure to incorporate key terms and concepts associated with your topic. Refer to yourself in the third person so that the host can use the description verbatim for their own promotion or notes. Don't spend a lot of time drafting this first version, because we're going to be using AI as an assistant to hone it.

Once you have a draft, put it into an AI tool such as ChatGPT with the prompt *rewrite this description of a podcast topic to make it more compelling, using keywords that will improve SEO* (search engine optimization). Scan what the AI comes up with and enter further prompts as needed—for example, *rewrite in a less flowery style* or *rewrite for an audience of male millennials.*

When you feel you've tapped out the AI's resources, copy and paste the result into your writing app and continue tweaking it. AI is great for idea generation, but it will never understand your topic, your goals for your podcast appearances, or your target audience as well as you do.

Using this approach, here's what Matty ended up with as a pitch focused on best practices for podcast guesting:

Matty Dalrymple, coauthor with Mark Leslie Lefebvre of The Podcast Guest Playbook, *will share insights on how to leverage podcast* **conversations** *to establish* **connections** *with hosts and to build a* **community** *within the audience. Drawing on her experience as the host of hundreds of episodes of* The Indy Author Podcast *and a guest on dozens more, Matty* *will cover how to identify the opportunities that align with the guest's offering and goals, how to craft pitches that land interviews, and how to establish rapport through a know-relate-trust model. Listeners will learn the best practices for making a positive impact during their interviews, including tips for providing the best audio and video experience, and how to follow up effectively to benefit both themselves and their host. Matty will guide listeners through each step of the process, providing a **playbook** to enable them to achieve their goals through podcasting, from initial contact to post-interview strategy.*

In any pitch related to this topic, Matty would always include the terms *playbook*, *conversations*, *connections*, and *community*, since these provide a clear tie back to the book the appearance is intended to promote. In a pitch intended to promote his book *Wide for the Win*, Mark would be sure to incorporate that phrase in his conversation.

Creating a Title

Once you have identified some conversational topics related to your offering and drafted your description, come up with some intriguing ways of titling them. A topic based on how Matty's brief ownership of a 1946 Stinson 108 tailwheel airplane inspired her work on *The Falcon and the Owl* might intrigue a potential host, but a clever title will make it that much more attention-grabbing. How about "Turbulence and Twists: Suspense in an Aviation-themed Novel"? If Mark was pitching a topic related to his book *Wide for the Win*, he might title it "Beyond Eggs & Baskets: Scalable Strategies for Wide Distribution." (You want the titles to be attention-getting, but don't make them so clever that it's not possible tell what the actual topic is.)

Creating the Questions

Another useful piece of content to create is a list of possible questions that an interviewer might pose. This is a great resource to provide to potential hosts and enables you to think through your answers to those questions in advance. For example, Matty's questions for pitches related to podcast hosting for authors include:

- *What should authors consider before starting a podcast?*
- *What might be a red flag that podcast hosting is not for them?*
- *What should they consider when deciding on their podcast's structure, format, and medium?*
- *How expensive is it to outfit a podcast home studio?*
- *If a listener is considering launching a podcast, does it have to be forever?*

Even if the host doesn't use these questions verbatim, it will be a helpful indication to them of your areas of focus.

Creating Your Pitch Template

The content you've crafted so far—topics, descriptions, titles, and questions—serves as fodder for your pitch template. Having a template improves the quality of your outreach by giving you an opportunity to refine the content over time, and it streamlines the process, preventing you from having to start from scratch as you prepare your pitches.

However, a pitch that sounds generic or impersonal will quickly land in the "no" pile, so during the pitching process, you will personalize each pitch (more on that in the section on "Making Your Pitch"). The key is to create a flexible framework that you can easily customize for each podcast and host, demonstrating that you understand their show and audience.

Your pitch template should include the following, some of

which will be common across pitches (e.g., links to your online platforms) and some of which you will tailor for each pitch:

- A placeholder for a **personalized subject line** – Your email subject line should be clear, engaging, and relevant to the podcast's theme. Avoid generic phrases like "Podcast Guest Inquiry."
- A **brief explanation of who you are**
- A placeholder for a **demonstration of your familiarity with the host's work** by referencing a specific episode, theme, or insight from their podcast – Authenticity matters; avoid generic flattery.
- A **description of the topic** you are proposing for the podcast, including a placeholder for a **personalized explanation of how your insights will benefit the host's listeners specifically** – Make the value clear and relevant to the podcast's niche.
- Options for **one or two related but alternative topics** – This gives the host flexibility and increases the chances that one of the angles will align with their interests.
- If available, links to **notable podcast appearances** relevant to the proposed topic – This reassures the host that you're comfortable with the format and can deliver a great interview. If you haven't yet guested on a podcast, provide a link to your demo reel, as described in the section on "Your Portfolio."
- A section providing **links to your website, media kit, and social media accounts** – Don't make the interviewer hunt for information.

- A **clear and simple call to action** – End with a direct and polite request, such as: "Would you be open to a quick chat to discuss this further?" or "I'd love to know if you think this topic would be a good fit for your audience."

Pro tip: If you use <angle brackets> in your template to set off the text that you will personalize for each pitch, you can search for those characters in your actual pitch communications before hitting *Send* to make sure you haven't left any placeholders.

Below is an example of an email Matty might use to pitch appearances related to coauthoring nonfiction. Much of this content would be consistent from pitch to pitch, with the content she would personalize for a pitch to Mark for an appearance on his *Stark Reflections on Writing and Publishing* podcast set off in angle brackets for the purposes of this example only:

Subject: <Sharing Best Practices for Coauthoring Nonfiction with Stark Reflections Listeners>

Hello, <Mark>, I'm Matty Dalrymple, author of suspense and thriller novels and nonfiction books for authors, and host of *The Indy Author Podcast*. I've long admired your work, <especially your *Stark Reflections* episode with Joanna Penn, which sparked your collaboration on *The Relaxed Author*. That's exactly the kind of synergy I love exploring and encouraging>.

I'd love to join you on <*Stark Reflections*> to share actionable insights from my new book, *Collaborate to Create: A Guide to Coauthoring Nonfiction*, which I coauthored with M.L. Ronn (Michael La Ronn). The conversation could offer valuable takeaways for your listeners on:

- Finding and evaluating coauthoring opportunities

- Paving the way for a successful and enjoyable collaboration
- Best practices for assembling and organizing coauthored content
- How coauthoring is like a creative marriage

<I think this topic aligns beautifully with the spirit of collaboration and author empowerment you champion on your show, and I especially enjoy discussing this topic with experienced coauthors who can bring additional perspective and insight.>

If it's a better fit, I'd also be happy to discuss the other book I coauthored with Michael, *From Page to Platform: How to Succeed as an Author Speaker* and would be happy to provide some topics of conversation related to that book.

I've had the pleasure of being a guest on *The Creative Penn Podcast*, the *Kobo Writing Life Podcast*, the *Self-Publishing with Dale* podcast, the *Self-Publishing with ALLi* podcast, and many others, and I'd be delighted to bring that same energy and professionalism to <*Stark Reflections*>.

You can learn more about me and my work at:

mattydalrymple.com (You'll find my bio and headshot at the About tab.)

theindyauthor.com

Would you be open to a quick chat to see if this topic would be a good fit for your audience? If yes, please feel free to grab some time here: <*link to scheduling app*>

Warm regards,

Matty

Continuously reassess your template based on the responses your pitches receive. Matty always has her computer's text-to-speech read any email aloud to her before sending. This not only identifies areas for refinement but also is one last check to make sure no placeholder text remains.

Planning Your Timing

Once you have your copy drafted, you'll need to make another decision about your pitching strategy: the target timing of your interviews.

How Far in Advance?

How far in advance of the availability of your offering should you start pursuing podcast guest placements? If you already have a large, engaged audience, you can start promoting your book, product, or service before its release. This works best if you're already recognized as an expert on a topic related to your new offering. For example, if you're known for expertise in indie author book promotion, you might announce that you're launching a book on social media advertising strategies in six months.

This approach not only builds anticipation but also provides valuable audience feedback. If you originally planned to cover all social media platforms but notice strong interest in one, you might narrow the focus of your book accordingly.

However, if you're still building your platform, scheduling too far ahead may backfire. Without an established reputation or a tangible product, podcast hosts and listeners may be more skeptical of your expertise. In this case, it's often best to wait until your offering is available before pursuing placements.

The other danger of scheduling interviews in advance of release is that you may end up not being able to meet the commitment you've made to your hosts and audience, which will undermine your reputation for professionalism.

This is a mistake that Mark made. In the summer of 2024, Mark recorded an interview with Joanna Penn for *The Creative Penn* podcast about a book he was working on entitled *A Book in Hand: Strategies for Optimizing Print Book Sales via Signings and Other In-Person Events*. The interview was scheduled to air in September of 2024, and Mark planned to have the book completed by that time. But a series of circumstances pulled Mark's attention and priorities away from that project and delayed the completion of that book (which was further delayed by his involvement in *The Podcast Guest Playbook!*).

Don't announce a forthcoming book unless you're quite sure you can meet the announced schedule.

Focused Push or Spread over Time?

Once you start pursuing guesting opportunities, should you try to schedule them as a focused push or spread them over time?

If your offering will have a definite availability date, like the launch date of a book, you might want to group appearances around the time of the launch. This can generate buzz, and your appearances may benefit from the excitement you feel around the launch date.

However, a focused push can have some downsides as well.

From the host's perspective, a possible downside is that, since you will be pitching podcasts related to your topic, these podcasts are likely to have overlapping audiences, and the host of your sixth appearance within a short timespan may be annoyed that they were "scooped" by five other podcasts. This is why Matty is less likely to invite an author to *The Indy Author Podcast* around the time of their launch. (You can minimize this downside by preparing a number of different approaches to your topic, so that even if a listener hears you on several podcasts over a short period, you're bringing a fresh perspective each time, as discussed in the section on "Defining Your Topics.")

Another challenge of a focused push is that the reality of a host's production process makes targeting a specific date, or even a specific timeframe, difficult, and you don't want to jeopardize an appearance by being fussy about when your episode airs.

With the vagaries of episode scheduling, we recommend you embrace the spread-over-time approach; especially if your content is evergreen, maintaining a steady presence on podcasts can be more effective, keeping you and your topic top of mind for listeners over the long haul.

For Your Playbook

At the end of each section, we include questions for you to answer—capture your responses in the downloadable document available at theindyauthor.com/playbook. Doing so will encourage you to think through how the information in the book applies to your situation and how you will act on it. For this section ...

- What is your topic?
- What is your description?
- What is your title?
- What are the possible questions you'll provide to the host?
- What is your pitch template?
- Will you try to group your appearances around a certain date or spread them over time?

PREPPING YOUR PERSONA

Your knowledge and experience are only part of what makes you a great podcast guest; how you present yourself matters just as much. In this section, we'll talk about crafting an audience-facing persona that reflects your true self while also aligning with the tone, style, and goals of each podcast appearance.

For Episode 220 of *The Indy Author Podcast*, "Podcasting Playbook: Navigating Guest Opportunities," Matty solicited advice from past guests about best practices for guest appearances, and we share it here with you.

Be Yourself ... the Best Version

The most common advice by guests offered was, *be yourself*.

Here's what Frank Zafiro, the host of the *Wrong Place, Write Crime* podcast and guest on many others, has to say:

Don't try to impress. Don't try to sound smart or worldly or literary or coy. Just be genuine. For one thing, it'll help you relax, and a more relaxed interview is usually a better interview.

The other thing is, in today's world, there's a lot of noise out there. And I really do think that more and more what cuts through the noise for the consumer, the person you want to listen to your podcast appearance and buy your book perhaps, is when they encounter someone who is being genuine.

I think there's a huge backlash when it comes to all the artifice that goes into influencers, and it seems to be trending towards those who are the most genuine. So be yourself. You're more likely to connect with a listener that way and they're more likely to become a reader.

To Frank's excellent advice, we'd add, *be the best version of yourself.* This doesn't mean presenting a false version of yourself, but it does mean remembering the three Ps of rapport-building—professionalism, preparedness, and politeness—which we discuss in more detail in the section on "Building Rapport." If you let your personality shine through within these podcast etiquette parameters, you'll achieve the authenticity that Frank recommends.

Make It a Conversation

Here's another pro tip from Emma Dhesi, the host of the *Turning Readers into Writers* podcast. Emma's advice emphasizes a theme of this book: the power of approaching the interview as a conversation:

The most successful interviews, both from my own perspective as a host but also for my guests, are when we both approach it as simply a conversation.

So perhaps my guest has a book that they've come in to talk about and they just tell me in a very easy way about the idea for the book, how they were writing the book, things that they enjoyed about it, things they found difficult about writing the book. But they're just talking to me as if we're having a coffee in our local coffee shop.

And it's exactly the same for anybody who's coming in who perhaps has a product or a service that they want to let people know about. I like to do it just easy, gently, as if we're having a chat at a coffee shop. And that way, the conversation feels natural. It's much easier for people to listen to. And I've also found out that that is the way to reveal golden nuggets that my guests are holding on to. They don't even know they've got them.

When a guest comes on and they've got soundbites in their head and they've got messages that they feel they've got to get through on the piece, they can sound quite stilted because they're very conscious about what it is that they've got to try and get across.

But when the conversation is flowing easily and naturally, I get the opportunity to then ask a deeper question about something and take the conversation on a slight tangent. That's when my guests most often reveal the golden nugget that they've got, the little bits of information or the little bit of advice or knowledge that they have that differentiates them from anybody else who is working in the same field or doing a similar thing.

So my top tip for guests and for hosts is to have a natural conversation, and to enjoy it and get to know each *other because that's when the laughter comes, that's when the sparkle comes, and that's what's most enjoyable for your listeners and what makes them come back and want to hear a little bit more.*

So how do you be yourself and allow the conversation to flow freely?

- **Don't use a script.** The only reference material you should have during the interview are some very brief notes (we share some tips in the section on "Preparing for Your Interview"). Ideally, as you become more comfortable with the interview process, you can discard even these.
- **Follow where the host leads** (within reason). The host knows the audience better than you do and has a better sense of what they will find most engaging. (If the conversation seems to be veering far from the intended topic, it's okay to make one attempt to redirect it, but if the host persists in their direction, engage with enthusiasm.)
- **Don't go on the defensive.** Of course there are hosts whose interview technique is intended to put the guest on the defensive, but if you've done your research carefully, you won't be pitching yourself to those podcasts unless that's the experience you're looking for. The vast majority of hosts will ask their questions in a spirit of interest and curiosity; accept them as such.

Fake it 'til You Make It

Many creators are introverts, and although carefully selected podcast appearances can be among the most comfortable outreach opportunities, the idea of speaking, even to an invisible audience, can still be stressful. One technique that many of Matty's guests on *The Indy Author Podcast* have found useful is to adopt a "fake it 'til you make it" attitude: pretend that you're someone who loves doing podcast interviews!

This isn't about being inauthentic—it's about tapping into the confidence and ease you aspire to have. Just as fiction authors create characters with distinct personalities and motivations, you can create and inhabit a version of yourself who thrives in the spotlight. Imagine how that version of you would speak with energy and enthusiasm, and how they would handle unexpected questions with poise. Over time, this "performance" can become second nature, and you may find that the persona you once faked begins to feel natural.

This mindset shift can apply beyond podcasting as well. You can "fake it" when attending social events at creatives' conferences by stepping into the role of a curious and engaged networker. You can "fake it" when doing an author reading by channeling a version of yourself who delights in sharing stories with an audience. Eventually, what starts as an act of imagination can evolve into a genuine comfort in these situations—just another example of the power of storytelling, both on the page and in your own life.

Choosing Your Outfit

An important aspect of your persona is your appearance. At first, it might seem odd to consider appearance for an audio-first platform like podcasts, but the vast majority of podcasts now record video as well as audio. The host may not post the video (if this is an important consideration for you, confirm that as part of your vetting process), but many do ... and even if only the host ever sees you, it's still important that your appearance conveys a professional persona, signaling to the host that you are taking the opportunity seriously.

One way to convey your persona or brand is through your clothing. This might be through literal branding, such as a logo or, for authors, a book cover image on a shirt. Keep in mind that optimal framing of your video will focus on your face, with just your shoulders and upper torso showing, so your branding needs to be high on a shirt to be viewable in the video. Another possible branding opportunity would be a hat.

We recommend not wearing clothing bearing brands other than your own—you never know when a person or organization you have no control over may do something to besmirch their brand, and you don't want potential fans viewing the video of your interview days, months, or even years later to associate you with a brand you'd rather distance yourself from.

Clothing doesn't have to be literally branded to reflect your desired persona. When Mark appears on a podcast representing his nonfiction work or one of the publishing organizations he's affiliated with, he wears a suit jacket over either a button-down shirt, or a solid color t-shirt. However, when he's representing his work as a horror fiction writer, he might wear a T-shirt or Hawaiian shirt featuring a skull.

Another great example of someone who uses clothing as branding is Diane Vallere. Diane is the author of the Killer Fashion Mystery Series, and her protagonist, Samantha Kidd, is a fashion buyer for an upscale department store who has a special interest in the history of fashion. When Diane appears as a guest on podcasts, she wears clothing that reflects this style: a 70s-style head scarf for the seventies-inspired *Grand Theft*

Retro, a strand of pearls for *Pearls Gone Wild*, and even a pajama top for her Madison Night mystery *The Pajama Frame*.

Explicitly branded or not, wear clothes that make you feel physically and mentally comfortable. Removing a potential source of irritation or distraction is well worth the tiny bit of branding benefit you might get from a more elaborate outfit.

Once you know the clothes, or at least the type of clothes, you'll be wearing, test them out. Open a solo session on a commonly available meeting platform like Zoom and position yourself as you will be positioned for an interview. You might find that a shirt that seems modest when viewed in a mirror shows a little more than you'd like to on-camera. You might find that a waistband that feels comfortable when standing becomes restrictive when sitting. Adjust accordingly.

A few more pro tips regarding clothing:

- Solid colors usually work better than busy patterns, which can be visually distracting and can even cause visual distortion on the video; bright colors usually work better than dark ones and allow the camera to auto adjust its exposure level correctly.
- Ensure that your clothing complements both the color and style of your background, avoiding any clashing tones or mismatched aesthetics.
- Avoid dangling earrings, which, if you're using earbuds, might create a distracting clicking sound as you move your head.
- Avoid bracelets that might clack as you move your arms.

Honing Your Voice (Literally)

Writers are used to thinking of the voice of our work, but in this section, we're going to be sharing advice about your physical voice.

The goal of this section is not to equip you for a career as a radio announcer or voiceover artist. In fact, we think that advice of that type can actually undermine the goal of improved delivery by making a speaker uncomfortably self-conscious about their voice. But voice, along with content, is the primary way you will be connecting with listeners of a podcast, so it bears keeping in mind.

Warm Up (or Cool Down)

After Matty left her corporate day job and during a time when her husband was away on a business trip, she gave an interview and realized only after the interview had started that the only words she had spoken for several days were "come," "sit," and "stay" (directed at her dogs). Her voice was hoarse from lack of use, and for the first few minutes of the interview, she sounded quite croaky.

Make sure you warm up your voice in advance and have a glass of water available for some lubrication. You might use a cough drop ahead of the interview, but don't have one in your mouth during the interview. It will distort your voice, and your microphone might even pick up the click of the drop against your teeth—an especially unpleasant audio experience for listeners.

The opposite, of course, is a voice that is scratchy from over-use. Avoid scheduling interviews right after you know you'll be cheering on your child's basketball team, or use plenty of cough drops before the interview starts.

Convey Your Enthusiasm

Matty's guess is that most people are like her in thinking

that they sound way more animated in interviews than they actually are. Don't gauge your level of communicated enthusiasm based on what you hear in your head; gauge it based on what you hear when you re-listen to recorded practice sessions or your actual interviews and adjust your delivery accordingly.

Refine Your Tempo

We've found that guests who are relatively new to podcast appearances tend to speak faster, probably in an unconscious desire to get through the interview as quickly as possible. Matty also has a theory that people who listen to audio a greater than 1x speed might talk faster because they become accustomed to this rate. She listens to podcasts at 1.5 speed and listens to her own podcast at 2x speed when editing, and she has noticed that her tempo when recording the interview intros and outros has picked up and that she needs to consciously slow down. Speaking too quickly doesn't give the audience time to absorb your message and can also make you sound like those super-fast disclaimers at the end of commercials for car leases or prescription medicines.

On the other hand, super slow delivery, especially when marked by a lot of *uh*s and *um*s (more on that below), makes the conversation drag.

Listening to recordings of your interviews will help you adjust your tempo, and you'll get even more valuable insights if you ask a friend who represents the demographic of your target audience to listen to the recording. They can comment not only on your overall tempo but also on places where you might need to slow down when discussing a concept that they're unfamiliar with or where you can speed up when covering familiar ground.

Remember, It's (Mainly) Audio

Although the vast majority of podcasters record video of their interviews, podcasts remain an audio-first medium. That means that anything you convey only via body language will be lost on listeners. If you agree with something the host has said, listeners won't be able to see you nod your agreement—you'll need to verbalize it. If you find something the host says to be funny, the listeners won't be able to see your grin—allow yourself to laugh out loud.

The Curse of Filler Words

Awareness of the use of filler words is an aspect of honing your voice where increased consciousness can result in decreased effectiveness—the more you try to remind yourself not to say *uh* or *um*, the more frequently you may find yourself falling back on them, and the more nervous this makes you, the more distracted you become, and the more filler words sneak in.

Some *uh*s and *um*s aren't a problem. For *The Indy Author Podcast*, Matty uses an audio- and video-editing software that can automatically remove these filler words; she finds that if she removes all of them, the conversation sounds oddly robotic, and she ends up reinstating some of them.

The issue arises when they're overused, and we believe the most common reason people insert filler words into their conversation is as a way to let their thoughts catch up with their mouth.

The best remedy is silence. Neither the host nor the listeners will object if you take some time to gather your thoughts, perhaps when the host first poses a question to you, but even in the middle of your response. In fact, the silences convey that you're taking the question or topic seriously and are investing the time needed to address it thoughtfully.

Verbal Tics

As opposed to filler words, which speakers use to fill silence, verbal tics are words speakers insert into their speech habitually, and usually unconsciously, that convey no meaningful content.

One that can be especially aggravating to listeners is the insertion of *right?* after a pause and immediately preceding the next sentence. We're not talking about *right?* as a means of soliciting the listeners' agreement (although that, too, can be annoying if overused). We're talking about the scenario where the speaker speaks a sentence, pauses, says *right?* and then immediately jumps into the next sentence. For example: *Podcasts are a great way to find new listeners. ... Right?They appeal to people who want their information on the go.* (Space after question mark intentionally omitted.)

Another annoying verbal tic is one Matty has heard called "contrastive agreement." This is when a speaker prepends a response with *no* even when they are agreeing with the person with whom they're speaking. For example:

Speaker 1: *I think Charles Dickens is the greatest novelist of all time.*

Speaker 2: *No, I totally agree.*

The problem with this is that there's a millisecond where your conversational partner thinks you're contradicting them, which interferes with developing the desired rapport.

Speakers who use these verbal tics probably aren't even aware they are doing so, and as with many of the aspects of honing your voice, it's an issue you may only catch if you listen to recordings of your interviews. Fortunately, unlike with filler words, awareness *does* enable you to better control or moderate occurrence of verbal tics.

Don't Highlight Repetition

A pet peeve of Matty's is when a speaker begins the answer to a question with "again" or "as I said." When she hears this, as either a podcast listener or as the interviewer, her instinct is to assume that the speaker feels they've already addressed the question and that their interviewer hasn't "gotten" it or wasn't paying attention. As interviewers, we're sometimes asking what we believe is a variation of an earlier question to better understand the topic, but even if we really didn't "get" the guest's earlier response, hearing "again" or "as I said" puts us on the defensive, and for listeners, it may reduce rapport because they feel the guest it being rude or patronizing to the host.

If in your review of your interview recordings you find yourself doing this, consider what's driving it. If you find you're using it intentionally to point out to the interviewer that you've already covered that ground, be aware of the price you pay in rapport-building by doing so. Assume that the interviewer really *is* exploring a slightly different angle on the topic and respond accordingly. In fact, if the question sounds repetitive, you could even use it as an opportunity to subtly shift the conversation in what seems like a more interesting direction: *X is not only a good example of Y, as we discussed, but also a good example of Z ...*

On the other hand, if you find yourself using "again" or "as I said" as a verbal tic, use awareness to reduce their use.

(An exception to the advice to avoid "as I said" would be if the host or guest is referring to a conversation they had before the official interview started—e.g., "As we discussed before the recording began ..."—or if a speaker is referencing a catchphrase —e.g., "As I always say, three of the most important ways of building rapport are through professionalism, preparedness, and politeness.")

Lack of Perfection is Fine

Rest assured that you don't need to refine your voice to news anchor levels to be a successful podcast guest. In fact, some of the most famous and best-loved voices are far from "perfect": Barbara Walters' rhotacism (difficulty pronouncing "r" sounds), Seth Rogen's nasality, Drew Barrymore's lisp. Matty has a bit of a lisp, and it seems very apparent to her when she listens to recordings of herself, but she has never gotten any indication that it's unpleasant or distracting to listeners. If anything, something unique about your voice or even manner of speech helps ensure that you are recognizable. We've both had experiences of people who have never seen our faces recognizing us at conferences when they hear our voices.

The only way to gauge how effectively you're using your voice is to listen to your interviews (or your demo reel before you land any interviews—more on that in the section on "Your Portfolio"). Yes, like it or not, you have to commit to listening to your interviews—it's the only way to hone your performance.

For Your Playbook

At the end of each section, we include questions for you to answer—capture your responses in the downloadable document available at theindyauthor.com/playbook. Doing so will encourage you to think through how the information in the book applies to your situation and how you will act on it. For this section ...

- Record yourself discussing your topic and assess it for enthusiasm, tempo, filler words, and verbal tics. What aspects are you most pleased with? What is one thing you want to work on changing?
- What is a candidate interview outfit for your interviews, and does it pass the tests described in the "Choosing Your Outfit" section?

ASSEMBLING YOUR GUEST TOOLKIT

Now that you've prepped your persona, you'll want to assemble the set of tools that every professional podcast guest should have. Since assembling your guest toolkit is fairly low-cost and because the items it includes will be useful for purposes other than podcast interviews, we recommend you do this before you start pitching podcasts. You don't want to wait until you've landed an appearance and then be scrambling to collect the needed equipment and materials.

Choosing the Tech

When you first meet someone with whom you want to build a relationship, you need to consider first impressions. The first impression your host and audience will get of you will be through your audio and video presence, and it pays to have a professional set-up.

Of the steps you'll take to become a podcast guest pro, obtaining the tech is one of the easiest and, if you assign value to your time, the least expensive.

We don't specify makes and models here because tech

changes so frequently and because there are so many decent options in each category. Instead, in this section we cover the considerations for the various types of tech and best practices for using them. (If you are interested in the equipment we use, you can find a list at theindyauthor.com/playbook.)

Computer

Use your computer, not your phone, for interviews. The audio will be better (especially if you follow our advice below about audio equipment), and you'll eliminate the noises that often accompany someone manipulating a phone. Your computer connection may be more stable than your phone's, especially if you're using a wired connection, and its additional processing power will help ensure the virtual platform runs smoothly. Finally, the desktop version of virtual meeting platforms generally offers more features and controls than the mobile version, and those features and controls are easier to access.

Restart your computer several hours before your interview. This will eliminate issues such as degraded performance caused by applications running in the background; by doing this well in advance of the interview, you avoid having a system upgrade disrupt your schedule. (Matty once had to ask a well-known author to stand by for fifteen minutes before beginning a recording for *The Indy Author Podcast* because her computer was busy updating its operating system.)

Although computers are the best option for conducting an interview, you should have your phone ready to use as a backup; make sure it's fully charged and has the interview platform's mobile app loaded.

Microphone

Don't use your computer's built-in mic—it will provide a poor audio experience for your audience and production headaches for your host. Although some audio purists are dismissive of the use of USB mics, we find their audio quality perfectly acceptable, and in fact Matty and Mark have used USB mics—the ubiquitous Blue Yeti—for years. Mark even has a mini-Yeti he uses when he travels.

Earbuds

Using earbuds will keep your mic from picking up the audio of the other people in the recording and further improve audio quality. We recommend earbuds over headphones because headphones look clunky and undercut the impression you want to create that you and your host are chatting over a cup of coffee or a glass of wine.

Camera

We find the cameras built into our computers to be sufficient for podcast appearances. If you do want to up your game with a webcam—or if your computer is not equipped with a camera—just search online for *best webcams under $<your budget>* and include the year. You might also investigate options for using your phone's camera as a webcam.

Virtual Meeting Platforms

The virtual meeting platform (e.g., Zoom, Microsoft Teams, StreamYard) won't represent a cost to you as the podcast guest, but we list it here because it's a piece of tech you need to be familiar with. At a minimum, you'll need to know how to mute and unmute your mic and to turn your camera on and off. If you find out that your host uses a platform that you're unfamiliar with, download it and check it out in advance. If you find it confusing, ask the host if you can hop on the call a few minutes early so they can review the primary functions with you.

Fortunately, virtual meeting platforms are more similar than different, so once you've mastered one, the learning curve for using others should be shallow.

Even if you have used a specific platform before, open it on your computer well in advance of your interview in case there are any updates that need to be installed. You can also use this as an opportunity to confirm that it will connect to your mic, earbuds, and camera.

Make sure you also have the app installed on your mobile phone as a back-up.

Creating Your Virtual Presentation Space

If you'll be pitching yourself to podcast hosts as a professional in your topic area, you need to be able to conduct your interviews in a professional-level space. Creating this doesn't require a huge investment—just some time, care, and ingenuity to make your audio and video presentation as high quality as possible.

A Distraction-resistant Environment

No environment is going to be distraction-proof, but we can at least make it distraction-resistant.

Matty's usual workspace used to be in her den, but it was prone to distractions from activity in the neighboring kitchen and from her dogs. She ended up moving her office to a small room upstairs—the same room where she records episodes of *The Indy Author Podcast* and participates as a guest on others' events. Mark also uses a second-floor home office for interviews.

When you're about to sign onto the meeting platform for your interview, set your computer and any nearby devices to do not disturb. If there is a door you can close, do so; that should keep roommates, partners, spouses, pets, or children from barging in. The closed door also reduces any ambient noise coming from other parts of your home. It can also be helpful to pre-alert others you share your living space with that you'll be in an interview; and sometimes a simple sticky note, sign, or *Do Not Disturb* door hanger can act as a reminder to those on the other side of that closed door.

Audio

Since podcasts are an audio-first medium, achieving high quality audio is vital.

Spaces that absorb rather than echo back sound will provide the best audio quality. Choose an area with soft surfaces (e.g., carpets, curtains) if possible, or provide soft surfaces as needed. Matty tucks the top of a throw blanket into the top drawer of the dresser that's next to her recording space so that it hangs over the front of the dresser. Seagrass room dividers provide sound absorption as well as visual barriers. In Mark's home studio, books on the walls not only provide an attractive visual back-drop, but they also serve to deaden auditory echo.

When possible, conduct interviews on days and at times when you anticipate the environment will provide the fewest audio challenges. For example, throughout the fall, Matty's neighbor tends to deploy an incredibly loud leaf blower in the late afternoon, so when she has the option, she avoids conducting interviews during that time.

Reduce the chances of background noise in your home. For example, when recording, Matty puts her dogs in the kitchen, where they can't look out the windows, rather than in the den, where they have a clear view of the backyard and the "intrud-ers"—squirrels, deer, and foxes—that occasionally "trespass."

The Visual Space

More and more podcasters are making interviews available on video platforms like YouTube as well as on podcast feeds. But even if they don't share the video publicly, most hosts will record your interview with video turned on, so even if you're "only" sharing video with them, they are an important audience member. Make sure that your presentation space conveys your brand and your professionalism.

I'm sure we've all had the experience—if not as part of a podcast interview, then perhaps during a virtual business meeting—of a participant who appears in a space that does not reflect professionalism. Maybe they're sitting in their kitchen, with a stack of dirty dishes next to the sink behind them. Maybe they're sitting in their den, with a desk overflowing with untidy papers in the background. Or, worse yet, maybe they're sitting in their bedroom, and their background is an unmade bed. (Even if the bed is made, video shared from spaces identifiable as a bedroom is not ideal—it should be one of the most private spaces in one's home, and being invited in feels vaguely inappropriate.)

Or maybe people or pets are wondering through the frame. During one appearance as a podcast guest, Matty got so distracted watching over the host's shoulder as the host's cat let itself out of the room by turning the doorknob that she had some difficulty focusing on the questions. You want viewers to be paying attention to your message, not being concerned that your pet is making a break for it.

You want the space to convey your personality—but always the best public version of your personality. For example, the room in which Matty records *The Indy Author Podcast* and her guest appearances is a small room intended for use as a bedroom. It contains dressers, which seem more appropriate to a private than a public space. She uses seagrass room dividers to screen them off from camera view.

Make sure the space is appropriate to and reflective of your topic. Bookshelves can be an attractive backdrop for authors as long as they are neatly maintained (unless messily maintained is more in line with your desired branding), and as long as you vet the titles that will be visible to viewers. If your topic is gardening advice, having some plants in the backdrop will be helpful ... as long as they're healthy.

How about a virtual background? They are getting better, and a powerful computer helps avoid the ghosting effect of elements appearing or disappearing as they move toward or away from the camera. Using a green screen helps eliminate the effect of an unnatural-looking border between the actual presenter and the virtual background. However, we recommend virtual backgrounds only if your circumstances make creating an appropriate actual background impossible. Except in the ideal circumstances, they can look fake, which is a distraction. Lack of a green screen or an underpowered computer may mean that when you hold up your book for the host and video audience to see, you need to fidget with it to find a position where it's visible. Just as important, your audience wants to get to know you, and a fake background eliminates one opportunity for them to do so.

Sit or Stand?

Should you sit or stand for your interview? Matching what your host will do, which you'll know from your research into their video content, makes sense, but there may be reasons to choose something else for yourself.

Mark always conducts his interviews standing. He finds that it injects energy into his delivery and is a physical reminder that he is "on" and needs to come out of his normally introverted self who is comfortable hunkered at his keyboard. Mark's standing setup has his microphone mounted on a swivel arm that he can rotate either into or out of the visible area of the video, and his laptop is positioned so that the built-in camera is roughly at his eye level. If you'll be standing, be sure to use wireless earbuds so you don't accidentally jerk your computer off the desk if you step too far away from it.

Matty conducts her interviews seated because she has found on review of interview recordings that if she conducts them standing, she shifts around a lot, which can be distracting for viewers. Also, if standing for the duration of the interview will be uncomfortable for you, be seated.

If you find you're going to be sitting for some appearances

and standing for others, it greatly eases your set-up if you have an adjustable-height desk.

Pro Tip: The controls for Matty's adjustable-height desk are positioned right where she rests her mouse hand, and on a couple of occasions, she accidentally activated them during an interview. The desk doesn't have an on-off switch, and it was awkward to unplug and replug it, so she got an auxiliary on/off power switch to plug it into so she could easily have the power off except when she wanted to make height adjustments.

The Lighting

The correct lighting is something that will set you apart from many other guests and even hosts, who are almost always under-lit, often because the camera is auto-adjusting to a brighter background.

Natural light is usually the most attractive and the most flattering light, but make sure you can adjust the amount of natural light coming in the room with curtains or shades.

Supplement the natural light, especially on your face. (What seems over-bright to you will look just right on camera.) If you have spare household lights, experiment with these before investing in presentation-specific lights like ring lights. Experiment with placement to avoid casting unflattering shadows. Experiment with intensity by tilting or even removing a lampshade—you'll need more light to achieve a noticeable effect in a bright environment than in a darker one. If you're using presentation-specific lighting, experiment with the color temperature—warmer (redder) or cooler (bluer).

Make an adjustment and then wait a few seconds to allow your camera to auto-adjust to the new setting.

Unlike some other aspects of your presentation space, lighting is not a set-it-and-forget-it aspect. Unless you're recording in a windowless room, you'll need to accommodate the changing light depending on weather and time of day. Be sure to give yourself a few minutes before each interview to adjust the lighting as needed.

Matty's lighting set-up is fairly basic. A south-facing window to her left has a curtain she can adjust as needed. There is a ceiling light slightly behind her, a small desk lamp on either side of her computer, and two mini ring lights attached to the top of her auxiliary monitor. Lighting in the background provides visual interest but is dim enough not to interfere with the camera's auto settings.

Mark's lighting setup is more elaborate, influenced by his background in theatrical lighting design. A large window to his left lets in harsh afternoon light, creating unflattering shadows and reflections from passing cars. To control this, he installed a room-darkening blind, usually covering 70% of the window to allow only indirect light. On very bright days, he lowers it completely. His ceiling light, positioned slightly in front and to the left of where he stands, would cast a harsh shadow, so he uses a dimmable bulb set to 40% brightness with a soft white or warm yellow hue. For his "horror author" brand, he sometimes changes it to red or blue. To his right, a desktop lamp on a filing cabinet bounces soft white light off the wall and ceiling. A mini-USB ring light, positioned behind his laptop, adds a soft yellow glow at 50% brightness. This setup ensures even lighting with no harsh shadows on his face.

The Props

Consider how you can use décor or "props" to support your message and your brand. For example, the space where Matty records episodes of *The Indy Author Podcast* includes a poster of a boat under sail, supporting her branding of the podcast's focus as "the writing *craft* and the publishing *voyage*." During the launch of her novel *The Falcon and the Owl*, she added an ironwood owl statue to her background (and liked it so much that she never removed it).

Mark's backdrop includes floor-to-ceiling bookshelves. The books immediately behind Mark are part of his "vanity display": his books as well as anthologies that his short stories appear in. Beside those are the hundreds of signed books he has collected over the years. Depending on the topic, he can quickly and easily reach for one of the books without leaving the camera, which has come in handy when the host asks a question that requires an on-the-spot look up. Beside the shelves is a decorative skull and crossbones and a sign that reads *Danger: Author at work*. It's on brand, especially as a horror author and as someone who offers advice to the writing and publishing community. After all, being an author himself adds to the authenticity of what he's doing to help other authors. A slight turn of Mark's laptop can hide the skull décor and place him in the middle of a bookshelf-only backdrop. He can even remove his regular wall decoration and replace it with something else that might be fitting for the theme.

Also make sure you've assessed the "accidental" props as well as the intentional ones. Matty often reads in the room where she podcasts, and she leaves her book on the table that is visible in the background. If she were reading an art book on nudes in modern art, she probably wouldn't want that in the background while she chatted with podcast guests. While Mark often has his dog Indie sleeping on the floor beside him while he is doing interviews, he usually keeps the door closed so that the cats don't wander in, as they can quickly become distracting accidental props who jump up onto the desktop, usually tail end toward the camera.

Refining Your Virtual Presence

The virtual interactions enabled by podcasts bring huge benefits —primarily the ability to connect with people regardless of geography and to do it easily and inexpensively. The downside is the potential for "virtual" to become "impersonal," but there are steps you can take to mimic in-person interactions.

Most podcast hosts want their guests to think of their interaction less as a job interview, and definitely less as a sales pitch, and more as a chat over your beverage of choice—hence our emphasis on *conversations* in the subtitle of this book. And these tips apply even if the host doesn't plan to publish the video but has their camera turned on during the interview. You and the host benefit by making the interaction conversational even if the audience only hears and never sees your interaction.

Here are our tips on how to mimic that chat-over-coffee-or-wine vibe as much as the virtual environment allows.

Place your camera at eye level. Positioning your camera slightly high is usually fine—in fact, it can have the benefit of encouraging you to sit up straighter—but positioning it below eye level is usually an unflattering angle. This is especially problematic when the person leans over the camera, as they might if using a tablet or phone, which creates a disconcerting looming effect.

Adjust your framing. A lot of people center their camera on their eyes, but that means the viewer gets to see a lot more of the wall behind you—or even your ceiling—than they need to. Other people sit so far from the camera that it's hard to see facial expressions or the cover of a book they might hold up. Instead, adjust your camera so that the top of your head is near the top of the frame. If you're sitting, as Matty does, this means that your body will be visible to about armpit level—think about how newscasters are framed at the news desk.

If you're standing, as Mark does, more of your torso might be visible. (In fact, if you stand back a bit, the distance has the benefit of making it appear, when you look at the visual of the person on the screen, that you are looking at the camera.)

Once you've directed your host and audience's attention to your face, consider where you want to direct your own attention.

Focus your attention. For presentation versus interview scenarios, the best practice is to look at the camera, because that will mean you are looking participants in the virtual eye. For interviews, however, the viewer expects you to be looking at your host, so that virtual eye contact can be disconcerting. But you still want to keep the audience engaged; how can you use your interview set-up to accomplish both?

- Select the view on the video platform that displays both your video thumbnail and your host's and reduce the size of the display window so that you can look from one to the other without too obvious a shift in focus.
- Position the thumbnails as close to the camera as possible—for example, if you're using your laptop's built-in camera, move the video thumbnails to the top and center of your display. If you're using an auxiliary camera, position accordingly.
- During the interview, spend most of your time looking at the host. This will enable you to pick up

visual clues. For example, you may be able to tell when they are especially interested in what you are saying—in which case, you might want to continue in that vein for a bit—or when they look ready to move on to another topic.

- Very occasionally, check in on your own video. You might notice that you're slumping and straighten up. You might notice that you've shifted out of your initial framing and subtly reposition yourself. You might notice that your expression, which reflects your concentration on the host's question, actually looks belligerent and adjust accordingly. But remember, although periodic check-ins on your video are useful, don't allow yourself to keep your attention there. Not only might it make you self-conscious, but you want to be focused on your host, not on yourself.

Your Media Kit - Your Online Résumé

One of the most important tips for working with hosts—from the time you first pitch them through and beyond the interview itself—is to *make it easy*, and one of the best ways to do that is to have an effective online media kit.

The media kit will contain everything a podcast host commonly needs to assess a potential guest, to prepare for interviewing them, and to promote the podcast episode. This generally includes:

- Topics and sample questions
- Bios
- Contact information

- Links, including social media accounts and past interviews or your demo reel
- Headshots
- Event schedule

We refer to this as a "media kit" rather than a "press kit" to emphasize the online nature of this information; we have never asked a guest for physical media and have never been asked for this by a host when we have guested on other podcasts. Don't waste time creating a beautifully designed PDF to be mailed as an attachment; instead, stage the information the host will need directly on your website in a format that is easy to copy and paste or, for images, to "save as." (We don't recommend sending a link to a shared drive such as Dropbox or Google Drive unless it provides unrestricted access; Matty sometimes runs into problems when a guest sends a share link to a restricted drive that she can't forward to the production assistant who helps assemble episodes of *The Indy Author Podcast*.)

We also advise that the online location to which you send hosts for this information be different from the location to which you send readers, since the information will be somewhat different. For example, you probably only want to present one version of your bio to a reader visiting your website, but you should provide several versions of different lengths for hosts (more on that in the section on "Bios").

However, you can minimize duplication of material on your website by including links to reader-focused pages on your Media Kit page when appropriate—for example, to book cover images or book descriptions.

In this section, we'll explore best practices for the various components of your media kit.

Topics and Sample Questions

As discussed in the section on "Defining Your Topics," you

want prospective hosts to have easy access to a list of the topics on which you're qualified to speak; share this information in your media kit.

For example, Mark might have both podcast guesting and the benefits of wide distribution as topics in his online media kit. Even if he was pitching an appearance related to podcast guesting, a prospective host who wasn't interested in that topic might have their interest piqued by the publishing wide topic. Furthermore, they might be interested in a specific angle on that topic: for example, understanding distribution options for ebook, print, and audio. Providing options for your host increases your chances of landing a gig.

Be intentional about the themes you present in your media kit. If you have expertise in multiple, unrelated areas—say, publishing and dog training—avoid listing those topics together. Instead, create separate topic lists (and consider maintaining separate websites or platforms) for each area of expertise. This helps position you as a credible authority in each field, rather than giving the impression of being a jack of all trades, master of none.

Bios

Your media kit should also include your bio, but not just one. Hosts will want bios of different lengths for different purposes—for example, a long bio to be able to assess whether you're a good match for their podcast, a short bio to introduce you at the beginning of your interview, and a medium-length bio to use in the episode's show notes.

What should you include in your bios?

All Bios

- Phonetic representation of any proper names that might trip up the host—for example, *DAL-rim-ple* or *le-FAVE*

- Book title(s) – If you have one or two books, include the titles. If you have a series, include the series name, perhaps including the name of the first book (e.g., "Matty Dalrymple (*DAL-rim-ple*) is the author of the Ann Kinnear Suspense Novels series, starting with *THE SENSE OF DEATH* ..."). (Why render the book titles in all caps and italics? Hosts will copy-and-paste text out of your bio, and formatting does not always carry forward, so applying both italics and caps to book titles means that even if the italics drop out, the title will still stand out from the rest of the text.) If you have several series, dispense with the first-in-series titles.

- Any special branding – If you have a tagline or branding phrase, make sure you include that—for example, when Matty references her work with The Indy Author, she always mentions *the writing craft and the publishing voyage*, capitalizing on her love of nautical metaphors.

Short / Intro Bio

Hosts will generally use your short bio to introduce you at the start of your interview. It can be tempting to include all one's books, awards, and other accolades, but remember that every second the host spends reading your bio delays by a second when their audience gets to hear from you. The benefit of a snappy short bio becomes especially evident if the host reads your bio while you're on-air or on-camera—you'll have to sit through that recitation, and I've seen guests begin to fidget or look uncomfortable or even embarrassed if the bio that they've provided drags on too long.

Here is an example of the short bio Matty would give to a

host for a podcast interview focused on podcasting for authors (~60 words):

Matty Dalrymple (DAL-rim-ple) is the author of the Ann Kinnear (kin-NEAR) Suspense Novels and Suspense Shorts and the Lizzy Ballard Thrillers and is a member of International Thriller Writers and Sisters in Crime. She also podcasts, writes, speaks, and consults on the writing craft and the publishing voyage as The Indy Author, and serves as the Campaigns Manager for the Alliance of Independent Authors.

The short bio shouldn't be longer than about 20 seconds. (Don't estimate this—read it out loud and time it.)

Modify your short bio based on the specific circumstances. For example, if this was for a guest appearance on a podcast aimed at short fiction writers, Matty would include the fact she has a coauthored book with Mark Lefebvre, *Taking the Short Tack*, that includes advice on how to create income and connect with readers using short fiction.

Medium / Show Notes Bio

A common use for the medium-length bio is for the episode's show notes, and this can include a more detailed listing of your book titles (within reason—if you're a super-prolific writer, limit the list to a dozen). You can also add details like organizational affiliations and, since this will generally be accessed online, links to your virtual home base, usually your website, and your social media accounts.

Here is an example of the medium-length bio Matty would give to a host for a podcast interview focused on podcasting for authors (~140 words):

Matty Dalrymple (DAL-rim-ple) podcasts, writes, speaks, and consults on the writing craft and the publishing voyage as The Indy Author. She is the host of <#> episodes of THE INDY AUTHOR PODCAST and the author of nonfiction books for authors, and her articles have appeared in WRITER'S DIGEST magazine. She serves as the Campaigns Manager of the Alliance of Independent Authors. You can find out more about The Indy Author at https://www.theindyauthor.com/ and connect at https://www.facebook.com/TheIndyAuthor/

Matty is also the author of the Lizzy Ballard Thrillers, beginning with ROCK PAPER SCISSORS; the Ann Kinnear Suspense Novels, beginning with THE SENSE OF DEATH; and the Ann Kinnear Suspense Shorts, including CLOSE THESE EYES. She is a member of International Thriller Writers and Sisters in Crime. You can find out more about Matty at https://www.mattydalrymple.com/ and connect at https://www.facebook.com/matty.dalrymple/

Pro tip: Make sure any links you provide have a space before and after them (that's why Matty doesn't have a period after her Facebook links) because search engines may think that the punctuation is part of the URL, thereby potentially breaking the link and reducing SEO effectiveness.

Long / Pitch Bio

The long bio is generally used by the host to assess your qualifications and fit for a podcast appearance, so this might include a full list of your books and links to other resources, such as a list of upcoming and past podcast appearances and other author events. Also feel free to include some fun facts that will pique the host's attention. For example, during the launch of her aviation-themed Ann Kinnear Suspense Novel *The Falcon and the Owl*, Matty included in her long bio the fact that she was once the owner of a 1946 Stinson 108 high-wing tail-wheel airplane.

Because your long bio will be, well, *long*, make sure to format it in a way that will make it easy for the host to find the information they're looking for. For example, they may not be overly concerned with your full list of book titles but be very interested in your past podcast appearances related to the proposed topic. Use section dividers and headings to make it easy for them to home in on the information they need.

Although the long bio gives you a lot of latitude in terms of the quantity of information you include, you should review it periodically to make sure the information is relevant and paints the right picture for your prospective host. For example, early in her author career, Matty included a reference to an award that at the time she was quite excited to have won, but as her career progressed, she dropped it from her long bio because she recognized it was not an especially prestigious award. Make sure to curate, not just collect, material in your long bio.

The Guest Close-out

You don't need to include the guest close-out in your media kit, but it's verbiage that you should have ready and be able to deliver smoothly, usually at the end of an interview when the host asks you to let listeners and viewers know where they can find out more about you.

Don't list every place your audience members can find you! That will end an informative and entertaining guest appearance with a boring recitation of URLs and social media handles. Instead, send members to one place—probably your website— and ensure they can reach all your other platforms from there.

Pro tip: Don't say "www" before URLs; these are just wasted (and tongue-twisting) syllables.

Matty's guest close-out is:

You can find out more about the Ann Kinnear Suspense Novels and Suspense Shorts and the Lizzy Ballard Thrillers at MattyDalrymple.com, and that's "Matty" with a Y. And you can find out more about my nonfiction platform, where I explore the writing craft and the publishing voyage, at TheIndyAuthor.com, and that's "indy" with a Y. I'd also love to connect on Facebook at Matty Dalrymple and The Indy Author.

Contact Information

Your media kit should include an easy way to contact you. You can do this via an online contact form, but you need to make sure that you receive notifications of these contacts and, if notifications go to your email, that they aren't landing in your spam folder. (Matty is convinced that authors lose a significant number of opportunities because legitimate emails are languishing in their spam folders; she has a weekly reminder to check her spam folders on all her email accounts, and she recommends you do the same.)

To improve your chances of a host's response reaching you, you might consider putting your email address on your website page. If you're concerned about automated systems scraping your address, you can disguise it (e.g., *Matty<at>MattyDalrymple<dot>com*), although web scrapers are wising up to this approach and may still find it.

You might even consider providing your phone number. Our colleague Michael La Ronn actually includes his phone number on his business cards and can point to at least one circumstance where doing so led to a profitable speaking gig. Although Michael did convince Matty to add a photo to her business cards, she hasn't yet added her phone number; however, it's less because she's concerned about spam calls and more because she dislikes talking on the phone, even with people she knows. But if you're comfortable with phone calls, it might pay to include your number in your media kit; you'll be more attractive to those hosts who prefer to connect by phone. As with email addresses, you can disguise it by altering the format (for example, leaving out the usual spaces or dashes), with the same caveat about smarter screen scrapers as applies to disguising your email address.

Links

Even if you have included links to websites and social media pages / profiles in your bios, provide a dedicated list of links as well—don't make the host scan through your bios when all they want to do is remind themselves about whether you have a Facebook page that they should link to in their show notes or promo materials.

Providing these in a list also avoids the issue where, if a link is embedded in a sentence and is not set apart by spaces—for example, if it appears at the end of a sentence and is immediately followed by a period—search engines may append the punctuation to the URL, thereby breaking the link and reducing SEO effectiveness.

Provide the full URL—for example, https://www.theindyauthor.com/—rather than *The Indy Author website* with a hyperlink. This will save the host a click if they just want the URL.

And provide the links in list form even if you also include them in your text bio; this will improve the chances that your host will just copy and paste the full list into their show notes. Here's the list Matty provides:

Matty Dalrymple
https://www.mattydalrymple.com/
https://www.facebook.com/matty.dalrymple/
https://www.instagram.com/matty.dalrymple/
https://www.linkedin.com/in/matty-dalrymple/
The Indy Author
https://www.theindyauthor.com/
https://www.youtube.com/@TheIndyAuthorPodcast
https://www.facebook.com/TheIndyAuthor/
https://www.instagram.com/theindyauthor/
https://www.linkedin.com/in/matty-dalrymple/

Headshots

The advice in this section on headshots comes in large part from the book Matty coauthored with M.L. Ronn, From Page to Platform: How to Succeed as an Author Speaker, *adjusted to reflect the specific needs of podcast guests. Thanks to Michael for giving us the okay to use this material here!*

Hosts will often ask for a headshot they can use for show notes, episode promotions, or the thumbnail image for their video platform.

An effective headshot is an important part of your media kit, but you can use it in many other places—for example, as your social media profile picture, on the About page on your website, and even on the back covers of your books. It is a key part of your branding, so invest some time and careful thought, and be willing to invest some money, to make sure that it supports your brand.

Establishing Your Audience-Facing Persona

What persona do you want to convey with your headshot? If you write business books for corporate professionals, a studio headshot in formal business attire helps establish credibility. If you're a cozy mystery author, a warm, approachable photo—perhaps taken in a bookshop or garden—might better reflect your brand. And if you write memoirs or adventure thrillers inspired by personal experiences, a photo of you at the summit of a mountain or beside a bush plane in Alaska could convey the bold, adventurous spirit of your work.

Accommodating Multiple Personas

Do you have different platforms that require different personas? You may want different headshots for each. For example, Matty uses a different headshot for appearances focused on her Matty Dalrymple fiction work than for appearances focused on The Indy Author nonfiction work. The aesthetic is consistent across the photos: casual poses and casual clothing in outdoor settings. However, the details vary: darker clothing and a more serious expression for the fiction persona than the nonfiction persona.

Mark's different brands—ambassador to the writing and publishing worlds on one hand, horror writer on the other, are even more distinctive. The more business-of-publishing-oriented author photos of Mark feature him wearing a sports coat over a button-down dress shirt, and he has photos with several different color schemes to choose from. When he's reflecting his horror writer persona, he's dressed less formally, maybe in a shirt featuring a skull theme.

And even if you don't have disparate brands to accommodate, having a few options gives hosts choices when they're selecting an image for promoting your episode.

What Not to Do

- Don't provide your host with a headshot that uses unusual framing—for example, an extreme close-up of just your features, or with your face partially obscured or out-of-frame. Such pictures pose challenges for the host. For example, the video thumbnails and promo images for Matty's podcast feature her headshot and the guest's headshot, and if they aren't generally similar, or can be made so with some easy photo editing, the effect is odd. Similarly, if the host is creating one image that includes multiple guests' headshots, as they might do at the end of a season, they will want the images to have a relatively consistent look across the images.

- For the same reason, provide an option for your headshot in color, even if for branding reasons you usually publish it in black-and-white.
- Don't confuse a professional headshot with a social media profile image. A picture of your pet or your kids, or of a cartoonized version of yourself, does not count as a headshot.

Best Practices

- As the name suggests, a headshot should be a relatively tightly cropped photo of your head, neck, and shoulders. Although you might have a full body shot for other purposes, podcast hosts will almost always want to focus on your face, and enlarging a full body image into a true *head*shot might result in degraded image quality.
- Have both high resolution and low-resolution images available.
- Provide your image in .jpg format, which any host will be able to access and manipulate.
- When naming your headshot image, don't call it *Headshot*—imagine the annoyance of a host who has to sort through the files in their Downloads folder trying to guess whose headshot is whose. Include

not only your name but also a reference to the orientation and cropping and resolution—e.g., *Dalrymple Headshot Portrait Tight High Res* or *Dalrymple Headshot Landscape Wide Low Res*.

- Avoid giving only the podcast host access to an access-restricted drive for your headshot; this will cause issues if they have someone else helping them with the production of the podcast.
- Of course you should always comply with a host's instructions for how you provide the materials they request, but Matty has found that the easiest way to accommodate providing a headshot is to provide the URL of the website page where she has these images loaded and that includes instructions to right click and *Save Image As*. She has never gotten any push-back on this approach and, in fact, this is how she requests headshots from her guests. However, if a host asks you to email them an image as an attachment, do that.

Levels of Professionalism

In this section, we consider some questions you might have about the level of professionalism required for your headshot.

Can I use a selfie?

If you reach the terminus of the Appalachian Trail at the end of your hike and find no one there to snap your photo, a selfie is completely acceptable. In fact, it might be the best option for representing the solo nature of the effort.

However, this example is a rare exception to what we recommend as a best practice regarding headshots: no selfies.

Selfies are fine for social media ("Here I am at the beach!" "Here I am walking my dog!"), but they are not professional, and professionalism is what your host and their audience expect from you. You wouldn't want to go to a fine dining restaurant and have your gourmet meal served to you on plastic dinnerware. You want your speaker brand to be consistently professional, and a selfie does not convey professionalism.

Can I at least use a mobile phone camera?

Mobile phone cameras provide quite sophisticated features, including auto focus, high resolution, and light correction. However, there are some effects that are harder to achieve with a mobile phone camera, such as shallow depth of field (blurry backgrounds). You may be able to mimic such an effect by using photo editing software to remove the background of your headshot and replace it with one more to your liking, but the effect may look artificial.

Results using a mobile phone can be fine, especially if you're on a budget, but they will never match the results of a professional-grade camera, especially one wielded by a professional photographer.

But professional photographers are expensive! Can I ask a friend to take my photo?

There are undoubtedly advantages to having a friend take your photo, and not just lower cost. Having a friend rather than a photography pro behind the camera might make it easier for you to relax, a key requirement for an attractive headshot.

However, unless your friend is a professional photographer, they may not be equipped to optimize all the components of the photo, like what effect different backgrounds will have and the overall composition of the photo. If money is tight, having a friend take your photo is better than using a selfie, but you will get the most professional results if you go to a pro.

Hiring a Professional

Consider the benefits of hiring a professional photographer:

- They come armed with a professional-grade camera and a host of other equipment such as special lenses, reflectors, and strobes that will ensure your headshot is of the highest quality.
- They know exactly which camera settings to use for every situation.
- They have an intuitive sense for choosing the right location for your headshot and the experience to suggest locations you would never think of. For example, Matty's photographer knew of a Blair Witchesque hut made of branches and twigs in the park where they were shooting her headshots—a background that was perfect for an author of suspense, mystery, and thrillers.
- They know how to position you to take best advantage of the setting—for example, posing you under a tree so that the light filtering through the branches highlights your face while keeping your shoulders in shadow.
- They can use photo manipulation software to edit out blemishes so that you look your best.

If we've convinced you that hiring a pro is the way to go, you no doubt have some more questions.

How can I make hiring a professional photographer affordable?

As with any profession, the fees professional photographers charge vary dramatically, so it pays to shop around. If cost is a consideration (and when is it not?), here are some ideas to make hiring a pro affordable.

- If you're having family photos done, pay the

photographer a little extra to take some headshots of just you.

- Poll your local writer's group asking if others need headshots taken or updated, then approach photographers with the offer of providing them with several clients at once. Since the photographer will benefit from the efficiency of the gig, they may be willing to provide a discount (not charge the same fee that they would for taking photos of all the participants individually). However, since there will be some set-up time for each subject, you shouldn't expect them to charge the same as they would for one person. Finding a happy medium ground will benefit you and the photographer.
- Anything that saves you and the photographer time will save you money. If you need multiple headshots for multiple personas, as Matty and Mark do for their fiction and nonfiction platforms, consider accommodating this through a change of clothes and accessories rather than a change of location.

What should I consider when hiring and working with a professional photographer?

Here are some things to think about:

- Get recommendations. Check out the websites of others in your local writers' group and, if you like what you see, ask those writers who took their pictures. You might even search for authors in your genre who live near you and see who took their pictures—a photographer's photos are often credited online.

- Get at least three quotes. To make sure you're comparing equivalent quotes, specify what should be included. Professional photographers will generally provide a flat fee that covers the pre-shoot consultation, their travel to and from the shoot location, their time at the shoot (including time you take to change outfits, for example), a digital contact sheet of raw shots (usually at least a few dozen for you to choose from), and retouching of your chosen photos (such as color balancing and removing blemishes). Make sure you tell them how many final photographs you want—for example, a serious version and a smiling version for a fiction and a nonfiction platform. Shop around to get the best deal.
- Once you have selected your photographer, get in writing an agreement on the services and deliverables to be provided. Matty was grateful to have a signed addendum to the agreement for her wedding photos specifying that she didn't plan to purchase an album, especially when the photographer forgot about that agreement.
- Tap into your photographer's creative as well as technical expertise. Let them know what kind of persona you want to convey in your photos; they can make suggestions for clothing and venue.

How often do I need to update my headshot?

It's disappointing to get to know your favorite creatives through their headshots and then meet them in person and find they look nothing like their photos. To avoid disappointing the fans you gain via your podcast appearances in this way, consider updating your headshot every two to three years, or more often if your appearance changes significantly, perhaps because of a new hairstyle or weight gain or loss. This schedule also avoids your headshot reflecting an outdated hairstyle or clothing. Don't use a heavily retouched photo because this, too, creates a distracting disconnect between your headshot and reality.

I hate having my picture taken! Do I have to have a headshot?

Yes, you have to have a headshot. The vast majority of podcast hosts will ask for a headshot, and you will cause them headaches and appear unprofessional if you don't have one. Any self-consciousness you have about your appearance in photographs provides an even stronger justification for hiring a professional photographer who knows all the tricks to relax you during the shoot, pose you in a flattering way, and process the photographs to highlight your best features.

What can I do to make my headshot the best it can be?

The best headshots are those where the subject looks comfortable and at ease, and the best way to achieve this is to be comfortable and at ease. Choose a location where you can relax. Matty avoids locations where there are likely to be passersby. Avoid distractions. If you're having the photos taken in your home, ask a friend to host your children at their house during the shoot.

The photographer as well as the surroundings will influence your ability to relax. When you're assessing photographers, consult not only the numbers in their quotes but also your gut— you're not likely to look relaxed if you dislike the person behind the camera.

Tell them what will help you relax. For example, Matty asks the photographer to count down to the moment they snap the photo ("three ... two ... one ..." click) so that she can smile on "one" rather than trying to hold a smile until her cheek muscles spasm.

And choose the clothes, hair, and makeup that will make you feel attractive, because knowing you're going to look great in your headshot is the best way to achieve a great-looking headshot.

Your Portfolio

One of the best ways you can convince a host that you would be an engaging guest is to share examples of yourself being just that. In your media kit, provide your prospective host with a page where you have assembled examples of yourself speaking on your proposed topic, ideally in a podcast.

But what if you're just starting out and you don't yet have these examples to share? Create your own demo reel.

A demo reel should be as close a representation as possible to a podcast interview. And because so many podcasts now include video, your reel should include video as well.

Apply all the tools and techniques we reviewed in the sections on "Creating Your Virtual Presentation Space" and "Refining Your Virtual Presence." Make sure your audio and video reflect the level of professionalism you will deliver in an actual event. Since you are pitching yourself for an interview, consider enlisting a friend or colleague to interview you. You can even provide the questions!

It's not necessary to stage a performance that is as long as the actual interviews for which you are pitching yourself; a demo reel of two to three minutes will give the host what they need. Use the first few seconds to introduce yourself. If there's an invitation you are especially enthusiastic about landing, you might even consider personalizing it for that host: "Matty, I'd love to join you on *The Indy Author Podcast*, and I've created this sample of the kind of information I could share with your audience of writers and indie publishers." (Of course, be sure not to share that demo with other prospective hosts!) End with your standard closing (see the section on "Bios").

If your demo reel needs some editing, or if you want to apply some effects like banners or overlays, there are many no- or low-cost apps that would enable you to do this (we like Canva), or you can find inexpensive video editing services on a contractor marketplace like Fiverr.

The goal is not to fool the host into thinking this is an actual event; it's to demonstrate your expertise in your proposed topic and your skill in and comfort with discussing it. The level of professionalism demonstrated by a well-produced demo reel will illustrate to the host that you will be an easy person to work with and someone who will provide value to their audience.

You can get the demo reel to the host by posting it as private or unlisted on a video platform and providing them with a link to access it. (Don't try to email the video to them—the large file size can cause problems.)

Once you've started assembling a portfolio of actual podcast appearances, you can retire your staged demo reel.

Event Schedule

Your media kit should include or link to your calendar of upcoming and past events. Since this list will be of interest not only to hosts but also to your growing pool of fans and followers, we recommend including this as a standalone page on your website, to which you can link from your media kit.

If you've accumulated a portfolio of appearances, this list provides an illustration of your experience and your professionalism.

If you're early in your guesting career, consider using as a placeholder a list of podcasts you enjoy. (Be sure to include the podcast of the hosts you're pitching!) As with your demo reel, the goal is not to fool the host into thinking that you've been on these podcasts; clearly label your list as "My Favorites as a Listener."

Give the page a name that is easy to remember and to say; for example, "Events."

For Your Playbook

At the end of each section, we include questions for you to answer—capture your responses in the downloadable document available at theindyauthor.com/playbook. Doing so will encourage you to think through how the information in the book applies to your situation and how you will act on it. For this section ...

- Where will you set up your virtual presentation space, and what modifications will you make to optimize it for your podcast appearances?
- What equipment will you need to acquire to reflect your professionalism?
- Which of the components of your media kit might you be missing, and what are your plans for filling these gaps?

IDENTIFYING YOUR TARGETS

Find the Opportunities

Once you've planned your strategy, prepped your persona, and assembled your toolkit, you're ready to find podcasts to pitch. Where do you find them?

Third-party Services

In view of the popularity of podcasts and of podcast guesting, services have sprung up to help potential guest find placements. One type the **online matchmaker** service. This type of service enables podcast hosts to post information on the topics for which they are looking for guests and enables prospective guests to post topics on which they would like to speak. There is such rapid churn in these matchmaking services that any list that we included here would quickly become outdated. You can find the current crop by doing an online search on *where do podcast hosts find guests?* and adding the current year. (We find that this reverse-engineering approach works better than searching for where podcast guests can find hosts to pitch.)

In the past, many of these services offered free plans that

included a limited number of contacts per month or a limited ability to post your guest résumé, and we would mention them to fellow writers as a "why not?" option. However, fewer and fewer of these services offer free options, and the fees can be steep. Another downside of using a service as an intermediary is that it reduces the incentive to do the personal research that will pay you back in more successful pitches to podcasts better matched to your goals, and more successful appearances on the interviews you land.

Another type of third-party service is **PR firms**. These seem appealing because you're capitalizing on the firm's experience with and connections within a space—ideally one well-matched to your topic area. However, the cost of PR services is even higher than of online matchmaker services. Another downside is that using an intermediary for your pitches makes it more difficult for the potential host to get a sense of you as a person and therefore more difficult for them to decide if you would be a good match for their podcast. Matty actually sets a higher bar for potential guests being pitched for *The Indy Author Podcast* by PR firms than for guests pitching themselves. And on top of doing the due diligence you should perform when paying for any service, you need to ensure that the service you purchase is not only from a reputable provider but also supports your goals. For example, a PR firm's contract might specify that they get you guest appearances on a certain number of podcasts, but this might incentivize them to place you on podcasts that aren't a good match for you.

We prefer the DIY approach to seeking podcast appearances, at least earlier in your podcast guesting career. In this section, we'll explore what those options are.

Your Podcast Listen List

We recommend that the first place you look for guesting opportunities is your own podcast listen list. As we've mentioned, the best podcast guests are enthusiastic podcast listers. To that we would add that the most successful podcast pitches are from listeners of the podcasts being pitched.

Obviously there needs to be a connection between your topic and the focus of the podcast—it won't do you any good to pitch all your favorite true crime podcasts if you write about gardening (although maybe ...). But assuming you like to listen to content related to your area of expertise, then pitching podcasts from your listen list will mean you're already familiar with the hosts, their format, their gestalt, and so on.

Your Fans' Listen Lists

Any individual can listen to only so many podcasts, so you may need to cast your net wider. Tap into your current fan base to find out what they are listening to. Obviously, this assumes that they represent the audience you want to reach and you are not venturing into an entirely different area. Knowing which podcasts your cozy mystery fans enjoy is not going to help you if you want to start reaching readers of action-adventure novels.

Online Searches

Open up your favorite search engine and search for *podcasts* plus your topic area and the current year. This list alone should keep you busy for a while.

Your Podcast Player Recommendations

Do a similar search on your podcast player and note which podcasts the algorithm recommends. Try varying your search terms and see which provide the best matches (and keep these in mind as terms you might want to include in your pitches).

If you click into one of the podcasts, the app will often display the podcast's subject area—for example, a search of "indie publishing" may come back with podcasts categorized by Books, Entrepreneurship, and Technology; you can use these to further refine your targets.

Colleagues' Podcast Appearances

You should be keeping abreast of what others in your niche are up to, and the podcasts these colleagues are appearing on to discuss a topic similar to yours can provide another good pool of targets. If your angle is quite similar to theirs, wait a bit before pitching your own appearance to a podcast where they've made an appearance.

Narrowing Your Focus

Your time is a valuable resource—one that should be spent on opportunities that align closely with your goals. Podcast guesting is a relatively time-efficient way to promote your work in comparison to other marketing and promotion strategies. However, the process still requires time and effort, so narrowing your focus when selecting which podcasts to pursue is crucial.

Instead of aiming for quantity, prioritize quality by seeking podcasts that attract listeners most likely to resonate with your message and offerings. For instance, as an author, landing an appearance on a podcast targeting readers is good; as a novelist, one targeting fiction readers is even better; and as a crime fiction author, one targeting readers of mysteries and thrillers is the best.

By strategically narrowing your focus, you'll not only maximize the impact of each appearance but also reduce the risk of burnout—promotional and creative—from overcommitting. Remember: your time is precious—invest it wisely.

Consider the Topic

Assess whether the topic's focus is **broad or niche**. For example, *The Indy Author Podcast* and the *Stark Reflections* podcast both broadly address writing- and publishing-related topics, so any topic related to a writer's work and life would be appropriate to pitch. An example of a niche topic is Jerri

Williams' *FBI Retired Case File Review* podcast, and you'd be wasting your time pitching to Jerri if you weren't a retired FBI agent.

However, don't limit yourself by interpreting the podcast's topic area too narrowly. For example, Matty's Ann Kinnear supernatural suspense novel *The Sense of Reckoning* is set on Mount Desert Island, Maine, and has as its backstory a fire that took place on MDI in 1947 that burned across thousands of acres of the island, including Acadia National Park and Bar Harbor's Millionaires' Row. If she were pursuing podcast appearances for *The Sense of Reckoning*, she could pitch:

- Reader-focused podcasts catering to lovers of suspense, mystery, and thrillers
- Writing craft-focused podcasts where she could share information on how she approached the research and how she did (and didn't) bake it into the book
- History-focused podcasts, especially those centered on Maine or New England
- Podcasts that explore paranormal phenomena (making clear to them that her experiences are fictional, not personal)

If Mark were planning a podcast tour for his humorous mystery novel *Only Monsters in the Building*, which focuses on a group of misfit monsters—werewolf, troll, vampire, mermaid, faerie, and werecat—who are seeking therapy because they don't fit in with others of their kind, he would pitch:

- Reader-focused podcasts catering to fans of fantasy, horror, or even mystery

- Podcasts that focus narrowly on any of the particular creatures in his book
- Podcasts focused on particular geographies: Upstate New York (the book's setting, at a remote cabin retreat); Ontario, Canada (where Mark lives, and where his main character Michael grew up); or even Canada in general, especially with a focus on Canadian writers / creators / artists

Consider the Audience

We've stressed the need to understand your target audience, and that principle matters even more as you refine the list of podcasts you'll pitch. Confirm that the value you bring truly matches the listeners that a show attracts. For instance, if you write erotic romance, don't pitch yourself to a podcast dedicated to sweet romance—the mismatch could leave listeners unsettled and damage your credibility.

Consider Recency

Check to see how recently an episode of the podcast has aired. According to the 2026 *State of Podcast Guesting* report from Tom Schwab's Interview Valet, less than 14% of podcasts have published in the last 30 days; the remaining are considered to be inactive. (Weekly episode airings are common, and podcast listeners have learned to expect this cadence.) Don't waste your time on pitches to hosts whose shows have "podfaded."

Consider the Format and Style

Podcasts come in all shapes and sizes, and it makes sense to factor in their format and style when deciding which ones you will pitch and how you will prioritize them. In this section, we describe some of these differences and the characteristics of each.

One-on-One or Panel

The most common formats for podcasts that feature guests are one-on-one interviews or panels (of either hosts or guests).

In our opinion, one-on-one interviews are the ideal scenario. You will get more airtime than with a panel, and you'll be better able to build a rapport with your host. That rapport is the basis of a connection that will pay dividends to both of you after the episode is a wrap.

Panel formats—a panel of hosts interviewing a single guest or one host interviewing multiple guests—also offer the opportunity for building connections. Be prepared to work a little harder for that benefit since it's a bit more difficult to establish rapport with individuals in a group conversation. Also be aware that the dynamics will be quite different from one-on-one interviews. When the hosts outnumber the guest, the focus is often on conversation among the hosts, and the guest can seem to be almost an afterthought. When the guests outnumber the host, you might find yourself sharing airtime with a mic hog or someone who otherwise doesn't understand the etiquette of panel discussions.

This doesn't mean you should turn these down, but you should adjust your expectations of what the dynamics will be and the benefits you will accrue accordingly.

Pre-Recorded or Live

Each approach—pre-recorded or live—has its own benefits.

With **pre-recorded interviews**, hiccups like your doorbell ringing with an unexpected delivery, the cat knocking over the microphone, or a sudden coughing fit can easily be addressed in the editing process. Even without a particular incident, the ability for the host to edit the interview usually results in a more polished product.

These interviews are generally more flexible timing-wise,

giving you and the host more time for rapport-building before the interview and continued conversation after the *Record* light goes off; this is when the two of you may identify those extra benefits each can offer the other.

More flexible timing also gives you a chance to address things like technical glitches. Live events are usually pre-scheduled to go live at an exact time; if you or your host aren't ready when the clock ticks down to zero, you're going live anyway. In one live interview Matty did, she signed on early to the platform and was chatting with the host when they both realized that there was a significant lag in the audio. They were seconds away from the scheduled start time, so they had no time to troubleshoot. Both of them were painfully aware of the danger of talking over the other person, so they were hesitant to reply even when they thought the other person was waiting for a response, meaning that the interview had many long, awkward pauses.

Live interviews offer benefits of their own.

They can be time-efficient, since they are usually scheduled to start and end at a specific time.

They are often part of a regularly scheduled program, which can often include a live audience, and the immediate audience engagement can create a greater sense of community. Comments and questions from live viewers can make the event more engaging.

Guest and host can benefit from and feed off of the feedback and the dynamic energy that a live audience brings. The nervous energy of knowing that anything can happen can bring its own benefits, especially if your audience sees you handling these occurrences with professionalism and grace.

Live events offer the audience the most authentic way of experiencing you.

Virtual or In-person

Interviews for the vast majority of the podcasts you will be pitching will be virtual. Although this has the slight disadvantage of making it a bit more challenging to build rapport with your host than would be the case for an in-person interaction, the benefits greatly outweigh this slight disadvantage. You can pitch yourself to podcasts on the other side of the globe as easily as to one hosted by a neighbor, and you only need to deal with the scheduling challenges of differing time zones.

When an interview is conducted in person, it is often at a conference or convention where the host has set up a temporary studio at the venue. Mark has participated in these, to mixed results. The biggest issue is with production value; for example, in one interview conducted in a noisy restaurant, while the content was valuable and engaging, the audio quality was so poor as to be almost unlistenable.

Conversational or Presentational

You'll only understand the interaction style of a podcast—conversational or presentational—by listening to some episodes. Once armed with this knowledge, you can go into your interview prepared to interact in a manner compatible with the host's style. Will they present you as an expert and then step back and expect you to hold forth about your topic (presentational), or will they approach it more as an informal chat over coffee (conversational)?

We prefer conversational style podcasts because this gives the greatest opportunity for building a connection with your host and for letting your listeners get to know you as an individual, a key component of community-building.

(If you prefer the presentational style, it might be a sign that pitching yourself as an event speaker might be a better match for you than as a podcast guest; check out the book Matty co-authored with M.L. Ronn, *From Page to Platform: How to Succeed as an Author Speaker*, for more information.)

However, despite any personal or professional preference

you might have for one or the other, you will need to be prepared to participate effectively in both.

Pitching, No Pitching, or In-between

Understand the host's guidelines for if or to what extent you can pitch a book, product, or service. Matty's guidelines for *The Indy Author Podcast* are that a guest will have an opportunity to pitch their offering at the end of the conversation, but listeners must gain value from the conversation whether or not they purchase the offering. Mark doesn't have any official guidelines for the *Stark Reflections* podcast, but he does make it clear that this isn't a podcast for readers, and what he is looking for over anything else is an engaging conversation that will benefit an audience of writers and give them something valuable to reflect on.

Even if the host allows guests to pitch their offerings, never let your appearance turn into an infomercial; serve the host and listeners—not yourself—first and you will gain the long-term benefits of connections and community.

Clean or Explicit

Some of the format and style considerations described above are just personal preferences of the host and might even vary from episode to episode. However, the designation of a podcast / episode as clean or explicit is a piece of metadata that the host must provide when they load their episodes to their podcast distribution platform.

Failure to comply with requirements of a clean podcast has obvious downsides for the host—they are likely to lose some listeners if the guest of a nominally clean podcast drops a few f-bombs—but the opposite can hold true as well. If a podcast is known for its raunchy language and you're not willing to match the style, the interview is unlikely to be successful. (You should be weeding out such mismatches during your research phase.)

If you're someone who tends to use profanity and you're

guesting on a podcast that bills itself as clean, then you'll need to rein in your natural tendencies—otherwise you'll force the host into some post-recording editing if the episode is recorded, or into some post-airing apologies to their audience if the episode is live. Mark has hosted guests on the *Stark Reflections* podcast whose very brand has been built around numerous f-bombs and childish banter, but when they have come onto his show, they kept foul language out of their responses.

If your natural style is more reserved and the podcast is billed as explicit, few hosts are going to complain if you don't offer up a few f-bombs (and your pre-pitching assessment of the podcast should weed out the ones who might). But feel free to expose this side of your personality if you wish. While Mark normally doesn't use adult language on his own podcast, he has adjusted his tone when on podcasts where that is the norm and expected by the audience. This works best if this behavior is brand-right; many of Mark's novels and short stories include characters using explicit language, so he's not wandering too far from his personal comfort level.

Edited or Raw

For pre-recorded interviews, or live interviews that are edited before being posted as a replay, it's useful to know how much editing will be done before they air. For example, if you confirm with the host that they edit their episodes, then when you feel a tickle in your throat, you might take a moment to get a drink of water, whereas if they plan to publish the episode raw, you might soldier through with a dry throat.

However, even if a podcast is edited, there's no guarantee that it will be edited as you expect; the host may include a bit that you assumed they would remove.

To avoid unpleasant surprises, to the extent possible, behave as if every interview will air unedited. If the doorbell rings, don't excuse yourself to answer it. If the cat knocks over your glass of water, handle it with aplomb (or, better yet, keep your cat out of the room during your interviews). That approach might cause a bit more stress up front, but it will avoid any unpleasant after-the-fact surprises.

For each of these format and style considerations, you might feel more comfortable pitching to podcasts that align with your own stylistic preferences, but don't dismiss those that are outside your natural tendencies. In fact, exercising the mental muscles that will enable you to flex to accommodate those atypical podcasts will stand you in good stead for all your pitches and appearances.

Assess the Opportunities

Once you've identified your list of candidate podcasts, you'll need to assess the opportunities. Of course, throughout the process, you'll be assessing them against the goals you documented in the Introduction, but there are other criteria to consider as well.

The Podcast's Popularity

Podcast popularity might seem like an obvious criterion for targeting podcasts, but popularity is difficult to measure. Publicly available statistics are unreliable—for example, if a report ranks podcasts within the huge pool of all podcasts ever created, rather than against the pool of currently active podcasts, it paints an unrealistically optimistic view of any active podcast's popularity.

You might try assessing popularity with an online search of *most popular podcast for* + your topic area + current year, but we can't vouch for the accuracy of that data. In fact, we both spend a lot of time listening to and interacting with the producers of writer-focused podcasts, and we see little correlation between such data and the success of the podcast in reality.

Never ask a podcaster to provide you with their download numbers—that would be the equivalent of asking a person what their salary is.

A great way to assess podcast popularity is to check in with people in your target audience demographic and find out what podcasts they enjoy listening to. A great place to do this is among your social media followers or your newsletter subscribers, who are by definition interested in your topic.

Listener Engagement

Another useful way to judge a podcast's desirability is to assess where, how, and to what extent they engage with their listeners.

For example, are they active on social media and, if yes, what is their followership like? This might start with an assessment of their number of followers but shouldn't stop there. Engagement is more important than numbers—if they have fifty thousand followers but never post about specific episodes, they will be a less appealing target for you than if they have one thousand followers and actively share new episodes, clips, or other content from their podcast.

Reputation

It's always a good idea to do a quick online search to make sure that the podcast you're considering pitching, or whose invitation you're considering accepting, is reputable. You don't want to affiliate yourself with a host who you find later is engaged in shady dealings.

Start out with an online search of the podcast and host's names along with *reviews* or *scams*. Also check our two other favorite sources: The Alliance of Independent Authors' Watchdog Desk at allianceindependentauthors.org/watchdog/ and Victoria Strauss's Writer Beware blog at writerbeware. blog/.

Affiliated Organizations

Checking out organizations that are affiliated with the podcast, such as sponsors or advertisers, is not only a good way to understand the podcast's audience but also to vet potential podcasts. Are they organizations you don't mind having your own brand affiliated with, even if second-hand?

Long-term Opportunities

Once you've decided which podcasts are most likely to meet your goals for your podcast appearances, a final consideration might be the long-term benefits you and the podcast host can provide to each other. Perhaps the host also organizes an event at which you'd like to land a speaking engagement. Maybe you're editing an anthology for which you feel one of the host's stories or essays would be a good match.

Make a list of your "finalist" podcasts—at this stage, let's aim for a dozen.

Prioritize the Opportunities

There is one step remaining before we dive into the process of pitching podcasts, and that is to prioritize the opportunities.

Take your list of about a dozen podcasts, and prioritize them: one-third as High, one-third as Medium, and one-third as Low. We'll use this prioritization in the section on "Preparing Your Pitch" ... although not in the way you might expect.

Once you've assessed and prioritized the opportunities, you're ready to move on to the next step of the process: making your pitch.

For Your Playbook

At the end of each section, we include questions for you to answer—capture your responses in the downloadable document available at theindyauthor.com/playbook. Doing so will encourage you to think through how the information in the book applies to your situation and how you will act on it. For this section ...

- What is your list of a dozen target podcasts?
- What are their priorities (High, Medium, and Low)?

MAKING YOUR PITCH

Every interaction you have with a podcast host either supports or undermines the value both of you can gain from your interaction. This rule kicks in when you send your first pitch and continues through the post-interview promotion and beyond. This takes time and effort and is one of the reasons that we recommend a targeted rather than scattergun approach for pursuing podcast appearances. You can gain more benefit from a dozen well-managed appearances than from a hundred badly managed ones. In the first case, you win fans and followers; in the second case, you leave a trail of disappointed and even disgruntled people in your wake. (And the podcasting community within a topic niche is a close-knit one, so you risk tarnishing your reputation even beyond the host you've directly impacted.)

In this section, we'll explore how to make pitches that will be successful in helping you build connections and community.

Preparing Your Pitch

Once you have refined your list of target podcasts (see the section "Identifying Your Targets"), pick one of the less well-known ones from your low priority list. Why low priority? Because you want to use these low-priority targets to refine your pitch before you try it out on higher priority opportunities. Remember, musicians don't start performing in front of thousands at Radio City Music Hall; they get their start performing in a local bar or club in front of a dozen people while they hone their skills.

The pitch template you created earlier (see "Creating Your Pitch Template" will serve as the basis for your pitches but you must always tailor it to the specific podcast and host you're pitching.

Tap into the research you've done to tailor your pitch and reflect your familiarity with the program and host. Matty is a sucker for any pitch that includes a reference to her beloved nautical metaphors for the writing craft and the publishing voyage. Mark favors pitches from people who demonstrate that they are familiar with the podcast and Mark's open-minded and reflective approach to aspects of the business of writing and publishing. If he had a nickel for every pitch filled with horoscope-like vagueness that could apply to any writing-related podcast, he wouldn't need to rely on the support of sponsors and patrons to cover his costs for hosting the show.

As suggested in the section on "Creating Your Pitch Template," pitch the topic you feel is most appropriate to the target podcast and offer one or two alternatives. For example, if Matty was pitching a podcast aimed at experienced authorpreneurs, she might pitch the topic of becoming an author speaker and, as an alternative, coauthoring nonfiction; she would not pitch the topic "Indie Publishing in a Nutshell," since that is more appropriate to writers earlier in their careers. (She would, however, include a link to a page that lists her full portfolio of topics.) The more different areas of expertise you have—as Mark has after four decades in the book and publishing industry—the more important it is to narrow your focus appropriately for the specific podcast you're pitching. Don't make the host sort through an overabundance of options.

Sending out your pitches one at a time rather than en masse and reading each before you send it—or even better, having your computer read it to you—increases the chances that you will find a productive way to personalize a specific pitch (and lessens the possibility that you will send out one that literally says, "Dear <name>").

Being Flexible with the Schedule

According to Interview Valet's 2026 *State of Podcast Guesting* report, in most cases, the time from introduction (a.k.a. pitch) to invitation is 0-3 days; from invitation to recording is 29-56 days; from recording to live is 29-56 days. That means that at the upper end of this scenario, guests can wait up to 115 days from introduction / pitch to the episode going live. With that much variability, it's almost impossible to target an airing exactly—for example, to coincide with a book launch.

Although it's fine to let a host know about key dates—for example, the launch date for a book you've written on the proposed topic—you will lessen your chances of a "yes" if you pose time constraints related to the airing of an episode. As author Melissa Addey says:

My tip for pitching to any podcast, reviewer or other media outlet is to be relaxed about when it happens. If you insist on the slot meeting your launch date or your timings, it'll be much harder for the host to fit you in. It's not just about the day it goes out; the podcast episode will be around for years, so play the long game and let the host know you're happy to be a guest whenever they can fit you in: you'll benefit longer term, and the host will be pleased they have someone flexible to work with.

You never know what's going on behind the scenes for your host that might dictate or impact the date of your episode, so be prepared to make the most of the content whenever it comes out —and, if the content is evergreen, for a long time thereafter!

FOLLOWING UP WITH YOUR HOST

There are three possible outcomes for each pitch you make: a no, no response, or a yes. How should you respond to each?

If You Get a No

There are many, many reasons a host might say no to a pitch, and if you've followed our advice (thereby eliminating reasons like a mismatch between your proposed topic and the focus of the podcast), the most common reason will be because their schedule is booked. Don't feel discouraged when you receive the inevitable rejections; that's part of the process. As in every part of this process, maintain your professionalism.

As an example of what not to do, let's take a look at the consequences of an unprofessional response.

Matty was once pitched by someone for *The Indy Author Podcast*. She checked out his YouTube channel, where he interviewed creators, and found that he had a standard question he asked all his interviewees; she was intrigued by the question and thought it would make for an interesting conversation to ask *him* the question he had posed to so many other creative professionals. She invited him to her podcast proposing that topic and sent him the link to schedule the recording.

When she received notification of the scheduled meeting, he had entered information about a totally different topic—one that sounded like an infomercial for his own offerings.

She cancelled the recording, which triggered a series of responses complaining about why she wasn't willing to continue to negotiate about the topic of the conversation. It's not clear what he hoped to achieve with those emails—if what he wanted was to appear on Matty's podcast, he wasn't paving the way to that outcome with his increasingly aggrieved communications.

If you receive a no (and you will—no one lands every podcast they pitch), don't complain or beg or ask the host to justify or reconsider their decision. Don't eliminate a possible future opportunity by behaving badly in your first interaction.

Commit to professionalism; just thank them for their time and move on.

If You Get No Response

There are a number of reasons you might get no response. One is that, in many cases, the entire operation is managed by one very busy person. Mark's *Stark Reflections on Writing and Publishing* is entirely scripted, scheduled, hosted, recorded, produced, edited, published, and promoted by a single person: Mark. He spends up to ten hours per week doing work associated with his podcast, and he is juggling this in addition to his work for Draft2Digital and Wide for the Win, his own writing, and many other commitments. In the process, pitches can get overlooked or lost in the email avalanche, and sometimes it's the first or even second follow-up that grabs his attention.

Therefore, don't underestimate the value of a degree of professional persistence, particularly when the fit for that podcast is a solid one. At the same time, you need to make sure persistence doesn't become pestering—don't be the person whose email arriving in the inbox elicits a sigh or groan from its recipient. How do you strike that balance?

Don't just ask the same "can I be on your podcast?" question over and over again; use your follow-ups to establish a relationship. For example, you might send them an email about a recent episode and describe how and why it resonated with you. (Ideally the episode is tied to your proposed topic.) Forward the email containing your pitch so that they can easily reference it, but change the subject of the email to reflect the topic of your latest communication.

Continued lack of response after a few attempts to connect is a flag that you should discontinue pursuing that placement.

Following Up on a Yes

You've gotten a yes on one of your pitches—congratulations! This is the start of what can be a fantastic connection- and community-building opportunity. How can you make the most of it?

- **Book the time.** Make sure you book the event on your calendar and include some buffer before and after the scheduled interview time for final prep and in case an interview runs long. This buffer also provides time for you and your host to chat and build a rapport that will stand you both in good stead in the future.
- **Alert others.** If other people—spouses, children, roommates—might be near your home studio during

that time, considering putting a meeting on the calendar with them as an optional invitee (e.g., *Matty live 7-8*) so that they know not to run the vacuum or engage in high-internet bandwidth activities during that time.

- **Reply promptly and fully.** Confirm the booking immediately; you don't want to leave the host wondering whether you're committing to the interview.
- **Follow directions**. If the host asks you to enter your bio into an online form, don't just paste in a URL to a page with that information. If the host asks for a 100-word bio, don't provide a 150-word bio.
- **Gather any information you need.** This might include confirming the best email address and perhaps even phone number to use in case of an emergency (and share yours as well).

If You Need to Reschedule

Any process that involves scheduling also carries the possibility of scheduling hiccups, and in this section, we'll share advice for when you are the person prompting the reschedule. (Cancellations, where you have no intention of rescheduling, might happen because you learn something about the podcast or the host that makes you unwilling to align yourself with them. These are so rare, and the appropriate way to handle them is so situation-specific, that we can't effectively address them here.)

The inconvenience of a reschedule varies from host to host —Matty and Mark both usually have four or five podcast episodes "in the can," so a reschedule is generally not a problem. However, if a host doesn't have other episodes recorded, then a rescheduled interview might mean a missed week for their podcast. If they plan to air the interview live, it's an even bigger issue (one of the reasons to favor pre-recorded interviews).

Matty's interview scheduling system sends out an automated reminder 24 hours before the scheduled time of the recording, and that reminder includes a link for rescheduling. In our opinion, 24 hours in advance is the right time to make a decision—you'll have a sense of what the following day will bring (for example, if you're on Day Five of a cold, do you generally feel better or worse on Day Six?) while giving the host enough advance notice to avoid inconveniencing them unnecessarily.

Some people figure they can gut it out but then realize as the time of the interview approaches that they just can't provide an acceptable performance in their condition, resulting in a last-minute reschedule request. A request for a reschedule that the host receives minutes before (or even after) the scheduled start time means that they have already dressed for the interview, set up the lighting, remediated their environment in whatever way they need to reduce undesired audio or video intrusions, reviewed their notes, and completed all the other minutiae needed to conduct an interview.

Do whatever you can to lessen the impact on the host.

If you're unsure what will be best for them, ask. For example, you might tell them that you're recovering from a cold and ask if they would prefer to go ahead with the interview or reschedule. Using a virtual platform at least means you won't be spreading germs, but you won't be in a condition to give your best performance. (We both prefer that guests reschedule if they're sick.)

If you do have to reschedule, be professional. Don't give the host a sob story; just apologize and make the rescheduling process as easy for the host as possible. As Michael La Ronn says, "Don't make your problems the host's problems."

If the host has to reschedule, recognize that it's probably more inconvenient for them than for you, and be empathetic to their situation as we hope they would be if the situation was reversed.

PREPARING FOR YOUR INTERVIEW

In this section, we describe the steps you can take as the time of your interview approaches to help ensure you give your best possible performance.

Revisit the Podcast

If you've followed our advice, you will already be familiar with the podcast and its host from your research in advance of your pitch, but it's worth listening to a couple of the most recent episodes close to the time of your appearance. Some podcast hosts have a personal update section or share personal news in their discussions with guests. If you're up to date on what's happening in the host's life, it gives you an opportunity to weave this information into your interview.

Listen all the way to the end! Matty was already a faithful listener of Sacha Black's *Rebel Author Podcast* when she landed a guest appearance, but she generally stopped listening as Sacha began wrapping up her interview with her guest. She was grateful that before her appearance, she listened to one episode to the end, because she discovered that in every episode, Sacha asks her guest to share the story of a time they unleashed their inner rebel. Because Matty knew this was coming, she was able to come up with an example that would be of interest and useful to Sacha's audience.

Assemble Your Notes

Assemble any notes you may want for the interview. You don't *have* to have notes, and the more experienced you become with podcast interviews, the less you will need them. If you do use notes, they should include no more than:

- Name of the podcast and host
- Your bulleted topic list (see the section on "Crafting Your Copy")
- A few (very few) other points you want to be sure to mention, perhaps ones specific to this particular appearance
- Your CTA (call to action), tailored to the podcast, host, and audience

For example, for an appearance on Mark's podcast to discuss podcast guesting best practices, Matty's notes might be:

Mark Leslie Lefebvre (le-FAVE), Stark Reflections on Writing and Publishing

*   **Topics:** *The importance of conversation to create community (readers) and connections (hosts)*

*   **Notes:** *Mention Mark's work on the Draft2Digital podcast*

*   **CTA:** *Free downloadable "The Indy Author's Guide*

*to Guesting Checklist" ... Pod Pro Author Coaching
service*

Your CTA might vary from interview to interview—for example, if you know that the host, and therefore likely their fans, are very active on a certain social media platform, you might want to direct listeners there, as long as you are active there as well.

Put your notes somewhere you can glance at them unobtrusively. A couple of sticky notes attached to your monitor near the camera is a good option.

If you'll be directing listeners to your website, double check to make sure that the information there is up-to-date and that all the links work.

Remember, these are notes only—*not a script!* Under no circumstances should you be reading from notes during your interview, unless you are explicitly reading a piece of your work, and even this should be kept to a minimum. Listeners have tuned in to hear a conversation, not a reading.

Prep for the Interviewer

Consider prepping not only for the interview but for the interviewer as well. As Michael La Ronn mentions in Episode 220 of *The Indy Author Podcast* "Podcasting Playbook: Navigating Guest Opportunities":

I want to know if the interviewer is going to be extremely prepared or if I need to help them with the interview. So for example, there are certain interviewers who do all of their homework and do an amazing job of making the guests feel at ease and steering the conversation to the guest's talking points. Other podcast hosts, not so much.

In those cases, I need to do some homework, and I need to make sure that I'm more assertive during the conversation to make sure that I hit my points and my calls to action. Make sure that you're advocating for your work and promoting yourself.

Refining Your Messages

You've crafted your generic copy (topics, description, title, and questions); now you'll want to consider what refinements you might want to make for specific appearances. You don't want to just rattle off the same stump speech whenever the red *Live* or *Recording* light goes on.

If a podcast has an online space for listeners to post comments, those can be a great way to understand the audience. Look for patterns in the comments, such as any themes related to topic areas listeners are most likely to comment on.

Also use the comments to understand the experience level of the audience—for example, are you speaking to a group well versed in your topic or new to it, and how might you need to refine your delivery based on this knowledge? If you are an indie author speaking to an audience of mainly unpublished writers, then you will probably need to explain what the term "wide" means in the publishing world. If you're speaking with experienced authorpreneurs, most will understand the term "wide" to mean distribution to multiple retail platforms, but if you also mean distribution via multiple formats, such as ebook, paperback, hardback, large print, and audio, then be sure to specify that.

Listener comments can also provide valuable insight into possible hot button topics. For example, guests addressing an audience of writers need to be sensitive about how that audience will respond to references to Amazon. Amazon has earned such a mixed reputation in the writing and publishing communities, especially among indie authors and bookstores, that any reference must be handled carefully. If your book is available exclusively on Amazon, you can mention that in your closing, but regardless of how wide your distribution is, don't over-emphasize Amazon—listeners know that they can get most books there (and if they *can't* get it there, the why behind that might be an interesting topic of conversation during your interview).

In general, heed the conventions of polite interactions of your audience's demographic. For example, Americans are often advised to steer away from discussion of politics or religion—unless your topic is related to politics or religion, of course—whereas this might be perfectly acceptable to other audiences. Older audiences may be less comfortable with discussion of what they might consider private matters than younger audiences are. Be sensitive to any signals the host might be sending that they want to steer the conversation in a different direction. (If you find yourself regularly deviating from host or audience expectations, it may not be a matter of changing your message but rather of reconsidering the podcasts you're pitching.)

Be sensitive to possible impacts of your topic. For example, if you're promoting your memoir about being an abuse survivor, you and your host need to be in agreement about the kinds of stories you can share, especially if the interview will be aired live. Even if your topic is seemingly innocuous—for example, pesticide-free gardening techniques—you're not going to want to discover in mid-interview that a pesticide manufacturer is one of the podcast's sponsors.

Also think about the larger environment of your specific topic; too narrow a focus can limit your opportunities and can even put you on the wrong side of your host and their audience. Mark learned this lesson the hard way, and his story is instructive:

When I was the vice president of the Booksellers Association, I guested on a number of radio programs, and most of the audiences I was speaking with were the CBC crowd here in Canada, which would be equivalent to the BBC in the UK or NPR radio in the US—audiences that are generally supportive of the arts and bookish endeavors.

One day, I was on a radio program talking about one of my standard topics—the importance of community bookstores—but what I didn't plan for was that I was speaking to an audience that did not respect books or bookstores or anything related to culture and arts. And that was a bad, bad error. Suddenly I found myself in hostile territory going, Whoa, this is not the place for me.

I should have gotten a better read on the likely audience in advance. For example, if I had known that the audience was interested in ranching and farming, I could have found parallels between the value to a community of a local independently owned bookstore and the value of an independent farmer or rancher. I could have started with something that drew parallels between a world that most of the audience was intimately familiar with and believed in and understood the value of, and I might have helped them see that that's what a bookstore can do. In a different way, a bookstore can bring a similar value to a community. One nourishes the body with milk and beef, and the other one nourishes the mind and spirit.

To that audience, I probably looked like a pretentious city boy even though I grew up in rural Northern Ontario. I could have found common ground by emphasizing my roots and my passion for the land and all of the things that are so critical and so important to that audience.

A lot of people in that audience were from an area

that is generally opposed to government control from outside. They're opposed to people taking from them and that benefit going elsewhere. And so I could have said, this independently owned business provides more money to the community than large corporations—about 75 percent of what you spend there stays in your community.

If I had done my audience research upfront, I would have been better prepared to help them see bookstores in a different light—as independent entities that bring value to a community, not just as places where the pretentious elite go.

That hard-won lesson leads to a simple truth: the better you understand a show's message and audience, the more effectively you can shape your stories to resonate with them. When you know what listeners care about—and what the host is trying to deliver—you can spotlight the parts of your expertise that line up, connect through shared values, and sidestep any pitfalls that could derail the conversation.

When Mark was a guest on the business oriented *This is NOT What I Signed Up For* podcast with host Ross Saunders, the topic was "The TERROR of Management." The entire episode was meant to help managers, and Ross brought Mark on to discuss his own decades of experience managing bookstores and teams within the book industry. When Ross asked Mark to share information on one of his recent books with the audience, instead of focusing on his horror or urban fantasy thrillers, Mark shared a little about one of his non-fiction books for writers and tied it back into the theme of the podcast, explaining that in this book, he boils management down to the importance of communication, networking, and connecting with other people. He finished by saying: "Whether you're managing or whether you're a writer, it's really about the connections—the human connections between people."

In all your communications, make sure the terms you use serve your audience. If Matty was doing a podcast interview about her aviation-themed suspense novel *The Falcon and the Owl* to an audience of pilots, she could use the term "FBO" and not have to explain it. However, if the audience included non-pilots, then if she mentions that two characters meet in the airport's FBO, she'd need to explain that that is the "fixed base operator," which is the business entity that provides services such as tie-down spaces, aircraft rental, and fueling.

It's sometimes difficult for us to identify what terminology is going to be unfamiliar to people who don't have our depth of topic knowledge, and the best way to identify any problematic terms in your message is to practice delivering your interview material to a good-natured friend who is as similar to your target audience as possible.

Tailor each appearance with this level of audience awareness to capitalize on your opportunities to build community and connections.

For Your Playbook

At the end of each section, we include questions for you to answer—capture your responses in the downloadable document available at theindyauthor.com/playbook. Doing so will encourage you to think through how the information in the book applies to your situation and how you will act on it. For this section ...

- What (if any) brief notes do you want to prepare for a podcast appearance that you've landed?

BUILDING RAPPORT

There are two aspects to making the most of your community- and connection-building opportunities, and we'll address these in the next two sections. We'll explore the more strategic approaches in this section on "Building Rapport," then dive into some of the more tactical tips in the section on "Delivering Your Interview."

At first glance, building rapport with your podcast audience might seem challenging since, unlike in-person events or even some virtual live events where you can engage directly with the audience, your connection to a podcast audience is second-hand: through the host. But since hosts cultivate an audience that shares their interests, goals, and priorities, you will automatically connect with the audience by connecting authentically with the host. Treat the host as a surrogate for the audience, understand their goals for your appearance, and trust that those goals align with what their listeners hope to gain.

The 3 Ps of Rapport-Building

Because alliteration is always fun, we propose three Ps as a way to build rapport with your host and, by extension, with their audience:

- Professionalism
- Preparedness
- Politeness

Your **professionalism** will begin with your pitch letter and continue through the promotion of your episode and beyond. By the time your interview begins, your host should already have had a great experience with you, and the listeners will pick up on the good feelings that experience engenders. You will further lay the groundwork for rapport-building through professional-level audio and video. Professionalism means arriving at your interview rested and refreshed and focusing your full attention on your interaction with the host.

Your **preparedness** for the interview will also build rapport. This means not only being prepared to deliver valuable information but also being prepared with information about the host and their podcast. Is the host knowledgeable in your topic area? If yes, tap into that expertise. If no, be prepared to provide more background information. Is there a backlist episode that would make a good companion piece to yours? Reference it. If you're familiar with the host from listening to previous episodes of their podcast or based on some other work they've done, mention that to them in your pre-recording / pre-interview conversation.

Before the recording begins, ask them for specifics about what they hope to accomplish in the interview. Mark has an example of delightfully surprising the host for his appearance on a podcast called *The Naked Podcaster*. The host records the interview naked (you can only see her naked shoulders in the video—any private parts are not visible or are blocked with recording equipment—and the title is a play on words, as "naked" not only refers to literal nudity but also to the idea of host and guests being willing to bare their emotions. Mark arrived for the guest appearance also naked (only his bare chest visible in the video, of course), jokingly saying "when in Rome" when the host introduced him.

And **politeness** is good policy in any situation. Here's a story from Matty:

I'm going to tap into a non-podcast-related experience where I was in the guest role to illustrate the practical as well as karmic benefits of politeness. Some years ago, I participated in an author event where authors paid an additional fee to have some time on stage to discuss their book. Because my appearance was focused on my Ann Kinnear supernatural suspense novels, during my time slot, I told a story about my husband experiencing a seemingly supernatural event.

One of the participants raised their hand, then launched into a long story about a time they had had a supernatural experience, and as their story continued minute after minute, I gritted my teeth and convinced myself to do the polite thing and not try to reclaim the stage.

I was glad I resisted because not only would it have been rude, but it turned out that the enthusiastic storyteller was also the owner of the venue were the event was being held, so if I hadn't maintained an attitude of politeness, I would no doubt have eliminated the possibility of being invited back.

Ultimately, professionalism, preparedness, and politeness are not just about making a good impression; they're about building lasting relationships. A well-prepared, respectful guest is more likely to be invited back, recommended to other hosts, and remembered favorably by listeners.

The Know-Relate-Trust Model

Beyond the three Ps, how else might you build rapport with your host and, by extension, your audience?

You may be familiar with the *know-like-trust* approach to building relationships, and while we agree with most of it, we suggest a slight revision. Allowing podcast audiences to get to know and trust you is essential, but rather than focusing on being liked, we emphasize being relatable. After all, there are plenty of podcast guests whose expertise we've valued—whose books we've bought or services we've used—even if we wouldn't necessarily want to grab coffee or a beer with them. What mattered was that they conveyed a sense of relatability that made us feel connected and engaged with their message.

In this section, we'll explore the ways you can establish a **know-relate-trust** relationship with your audience.

Let Your Audience Know You – Your Self-Introduction

"Why don't you tell us a little bit about yourself ...?" is a common way for interviewers to start their conversation—in fact, it's so common that it has two pitfalls:

- If you craft a single response and use it every time an interviewer asks you this question, you'll get bored telling it, and listeners who consume multiple podcasts related to your topic area may hear you on more than one podcast and likewise get bored with it. This is especially problematic if you're scheduling a lot of interviews in a short period of time, as you may try to do in support of a book launch.

- If you use a clearly canned response whenever an interviewer asks you this question, even listeners who have never heard it before may get bored!

Many guests' automatic answer to this question is a recitation of a short biography as it applies to their topic—and, in some cases, even as it *doesn't* apply to their topic. How many author interviews have you heard where the interviewee's answer to this question begins, "I started writing when I was a child ..."? When listeners hear that, they're probably already starting to tune out.

Why? Because they probably don't yet care enough about the guest to want to listen to the story of their life. More importantly, it's not clear what the story has to do with them, the listener.

As the guest, your focus should be on the host, the audience, and your topic—not yourself. If you do this effectively, then you will automatically serve whatever goals you have for your appearance because meeting your goals requires you to make a meaningful connection with the host and audience.

How can you craft your answer to this inevitable question in a way that enables you to build rapport right from the start?

Defy expectations. Listeners of podcasts featuring authors have become so accustomed to the "I started writing when I was a child ..." answer that they take notice when Matty starts out her answer with, "I had to spend several decades being a voracious reader before I felt prepared to become a writer." If her audience is mainly readers, she has already built rapport with them through that shared interest. If her audience is mainly writers, she describes the learnings she drew from a few books, which encompasses valuable craft advice. She also often discusses how her goal of becoming a full-time author was inspired by her father, whose short stories appeared in *Collier's* and *Cosmopolitan.*

Even if your backstory includes the familiar "I started writing when I was young" element, you don't have to present it in the usual way. Consider sharing a unique anecdote that captures a formative experience with storytelling or a humorous take on your earliest writing attempts. When Mark is faced with the question of how and when he started writing, he might describe how he started his collection of thousands of writing rejections at the age of fifteen and learned, the hard way, that a high brow literary contest was *not* interested in reading a macabre horror tale. Other times he might say that as an only child, he had to amuse himself by embracing reading whatever he could get his hands on—storybooks, novels, comics, the back of cereal boxes, the warning labels on his parents' cigarette packages—as well as filling the time by making up elaborate stories he would act out and perform using Fisher-Price action figures. A conventional question doesn't require a conventional response; infuse it with personality and originality to make it memorable and allow your audience to get to know you.

Let Your Audience Relate to You – Be a Storyteller

Once you've allowed the audience to know you through your self-introduction, how do you lay the groundwork for enabling them to relate to you? The best way to build a relationship is with stories, so go into the interview as a storyteller, not as a salesperson.

Storytelling is a vital part of a good interview. Writers—of fiction or nonfiction, by vocation or by avocation—have an advantage here since they can tap into their innate storytelling ability. However, storytelling for a podcast interview differs from storytelling for a book. If your storytelling skills are based on writing novel-length works or full-length creative nonfiction books, then you'll have much less time in which to tell your story, and it needs to be crafted to support the know-relate-trust model.

There are two types of stories that will serve you best as a podcast guest: those that are intended primarily to **engage and intrigue**, and those that are intended primarily to **educate and inspire**.

Stories to Engage and Intrigue

Stories intended primarily to engage and intrigue are valuable for interviews focused on fiction work. The goal of these stories is to captivate the listener, drawing them naturally towards a desire to explore your work further.

The default story to tell as a fiction writer might seem to be the story of your novel, but not only will this take way longer than you'll have in a podcast interview, but it's not what the host or listeners want to hear. If they wanted a synopsis, they would read your sales description.

What they want is the story behind the story—something that will enable them to get to know you as the author or will engage and intrigue them about the creation of the book. These topics might include:

- A personal experience or emotion you channeled into a character or scene
- A setting that plays a key role in the story—and your personal connection to it
- A question you were exploring or a theme you wanted to wrestle with in the story
- A research rabbit hole that led you to a surprising or serendipitous plot element
- A real-life person or event that inspired a character or conflict

- A creative challenge you encountered—and how you overcame it
- A "what if?" scenario that sparked the story's premise
- A scene or character that changed significantly from your original plan—and why
- An unexpected reaction from early readers or critique partners that shaped the final version

If you're having trouble identifying the story behind the story for your book, enlist a friend who is in a demographic that is similar to the audience you want to reach and have a chat with them about your book; you'll gravitate naturally to those stories behind the story. You gain the added benefit of being able to see their reactions and can adjust your stories to capitalize on the parts that are most engaging to them or downplaying or eliminating the parts that are least engaging.

When Mark talks about his thriller *Evasion*, a book that has been described as "*Die Hard* in an office building in Toronto," he shares that the inspiration for the tale came from a strange experience he had a few months after his father's death. He kept thinking that he had spotted his dad in a crowded place or in a vehicle driving by on the highway. He knew it was the side-effect of a combination of grief and wish-fulfillment, but that led to the question: "What if he *was* still alive?" And that led to other questions, such as how that might happen and what would cause it.

Often, when Mark shares this story, he and the host engage in a discussion about the loss of a loved one, sometimes with the other person sharing their own similar experience. This makes for a more relatable and riveting discussion that listeners are going to empathize with, since it's not a discussion about Mark's novel, but about a universal emotional experience.

Stories to Educate and Inspire

Stories intended primarily to educate and inspire are perfect for interviews focused on a creative nonfiction or advice book. The goal of these stories is to empower the listener, sharing insights and strategies that can add value to their lives and subtly illustrating how your offering can support their journey. Just as fiction authors shouldn't lean on a synopsis of their book's plot to relate to the audience, nonfiction authors shouldn't allow their stories to be rote recitations of facts or advice.

When being interviewed about a book of trivia he wrote that focuses on the John Hughes movie *Planes, Trains and Automobiles* starring Steve Martin and John Candy, Mark shares two important elements that inspired him to write the book. The first was his life-long adoration of this odd-couple buddy travel adventure John Hughes wrote after having a Chicago-bound flight diverted to Wichita. Mark shares a few of his own travel misadventures, including a disastrous road trip he had with his son, who was also a big fan of the movie, and how they posed for a selfie inspired by a popular image from the film.

The second was the fact that he is a self-professed book nerd who always pays attention to the books people read in movies. Mark's curiosity was piqued when he spotted a near duplicate of the book John Candy's character reads in *Planes, Trains, and Automobiles* appear in a *Deadpool* movie with Ryan Reynolds. That sparked his investigation as to "why that book?" Those two inspirations came together in *The Canadian Mounted*, Mark's tribute to Hughes's movie.

Most people have encountered their own frustrating and sometimes humorous experiences when their own travel plans have taken a wrong turn, so Mark's story instantly creates a point of connection. And it's likely that there will be at least a few members of the audience who are obsessed with movie props, whether those are books, music, or other cultural artifacts.

As with stories intended to engage and intrigue, chatting about your topic with a friend who represents your target demographic is a great way to identify these stories.

Keep it Fresh

Remember that even though you might have told a particular story dozens of times, for most of the listeners, this will be their first time hearing it. Keep it fresh! This can be especially difficult if you're doing a closely scheduled series of podcast interviews—for example, in support of a book launch—so consider this a reason for spreading out the interviews a bit.

The advice to keep it fresh applies to your answers to questions posed by the host as well as to the stories you tell. Something Mark learned from decades of bookselling is that when someone asks you a question you have answered a hundred times that day or that week—not uncommon in retail environments during the holiday season—it's easy to roll one's eyes and regurgitate the same tired answer. But it's important to remember that for the person posing the question, this is their first time asking it, and they genuinely do not know the answer. Providing them the answer with sincerity and compassion was not only a better experience for the person asking, but it also made Mark's own day more positive.

Similarly, a podcast host might ask a question you've heard countless times, such as, "Where do you get your ideas?" But this is the very first time the two of you are engaged in conversation, and they're asking that question because they are curious about the answer. It's true that writers find inspiration from numerous sources, but for those who aren't writers themselves, the concept of how writers make up the stories can seem somewhat mystical.

In response to such a question, science fiction author Harlan

Ellison famously said: "I always tell them, 'Schenectady.' They look at me with confusion and I say, 'Yeah, there's this 'idea service' in Schenectady and every week like clockwork they send me a fresh six-pack of ideas for 25 bucks." Other writers, inspired by Ellison's wry response, have provided similar quips. Stephen King once said he got his from a used ideas store in Utica.

Once you've refined the stories you want to tell, you can use them in situations other than podcast appearances—for example, for speaking engagements or to land a sale and win over a new fan at an in-person sales event.

Let Your Audience Trust You – Demonstrate Empathy and Share Generously

You go into a podcast interview with an immediate advantage with the audience, which is predisposed to trust you because you are being introduced to them by someone they already trust: the host. You'll use your self-introduction and stories to build rapport and therefore lay the foundations for trust. But trust-building extends to other aspects of your interview as well.

One of the first considerations in building trust is not just how the audience relates to you but how you relate to them. It's essential not only to know who they are but to show that you understand them: the challenges they face, the questions they grapple with. Sharing your own experiences with similar issues can foster a genuine connection. By approaching the topic at hand with compassion, clarity, and respect, you demonstrate authentic empathy, reinforcing your credibility and strengthening your bond with the audience.

Part of expressing this empathy is sharing content that your audience will value, but authors sometimes wonder how much of their information they should share in a podcast interview.

They worry, "If I share what I know, why will the listeners want to buy my book / product / services?"

The response could constitute the shortest chapter of this book.

Share generously whatever information you believe will provide value to the audience.

Let's delve into why we say that.

For fiction writers, this is less of an issue—no novelist is going to share the entire contents of their book on a podcast. But even if you landed an opportunity to read a novella in a limited series podcast—in which case, at the end of that series, you would have shared all the content of your novella—there will still be listeners who will purchase your book. Numerous authors, such as Mur Lafferty, Scott Sigler, and Terry Fallis built their careers on giving away their entire novels for free via weekly podcasts. Not only did that help them sell books in non-audio formats but it also led to traditionally published book deals.

Sharing content is a non-issue for nonfiction writers as well. We believe—and we've had our belief confirmed over and over again by fellow authors, author-services colleagues, and other creators—that even if you were to share everything you had put in your book in a podcast interview (which would be impossible), people will still buy your book. They might want to refresh their memory about a certain point or be able to refer back to it more easily than they could via a podcast episode. They might be someone who learns more effectively by reading than by hearing. They might purchase it as a way of thanking you for the information you shared in your interview.

You can rest assured that you are not cannibalizing sales by sharing information from your book in an interview.

The same holds true of services. If you provide coaching or consulting services, then listeners will be intrigued by the information you share in the interview, may buy your book for all the reasons we list above, and may still sign up for those services because they want personalized help implementing your advice.

However, we don't want you to interpret this as advice to try to shoehorn every bit of information you have into an interview —that's just going to leave you, your host, and your listeners mentally exhausted.

Think of yourself as a jewelry maker with a trunk full of your creations. You've set up a booth at a craft fair, and you're putting out on your display racks the pieces you think will be most appealing to the browsers at this fair. Maybe you make the decision based on the location of the fair—palm tree pendants for a fair in Key West or lobster pendants for one in Maine. Maybe you make it based on the demographic of the browsers— perhaps your jewelry references aspects of popular culture that will be meaningful to teenagers but not necessarily to their parents or grandparents.

What you don't do is empty the contents of your trunk onto your table. That would result in a jumble of product that will appeal to no one.

How do you curate what you share in an interview to highlight the content that will be of most value to your listeners? Tap into what you learned about your audience based on our advice in the section on "Preparing for Your Interview." And be flexible—if the host expresses interest in a particular topic during the interview, feel free to explore it in depth, perhaps at the expense of the other points you prepared. Enter the conversation with your host willing to go where their interest leads the two of you.

Approach the interaction with your host and audience with a service, not sale, mindset. Share curated, audience-focused content with a spirit of generosity. Engage in a conversation with, not a monologue at, your host. These guidelines will establish trust with your host and audience.

No Hard Sells

Don't undercut all the effort you've put into rapport-building only to ruin it with a heavy-handed sales pitch.

It's easy to get fixated on the goal of making a sale, but it's easier to illustrate the price you pay for letting this be your focus if we play out this situation in an in-person rather than virtual scenario, with you as the audience rather than the speaker.

Imagine you're at a writers' conference, and one evening there is a social event for writers in your genre. The attendees, including you, are like the podcast listeners: a group brought together by a common interest.

The event includes a guest of honor who is a recognized expert in your genre (the equivalent of the podcast guest). You approach the guest, eager to hear what they have to say about genre-specific topics—perhaps the approach they use for structuring their narrative, their feelings about the genre's common tropes and how to deploy them in the story, or their favorite books in the genre. (In other words, exactly the kinds of things a podcast listener might want to hear from an expert guest.)

Instead, as you approach them, they thrust a business card into your hand and tell you that they have a new book coming out that contains all the information you could possibly need to know. It might even include information on the topics you had hoped to discuss with the expert.

What do you do?

If you're like us, you find a way to extract yourself from that interaction as quickly as possible, and you certainly don't rush right out and buy the book.

Approaching a podcast guest appearance with a sales

mindset rather than a service mindset will make the listener reach for the *Stop* button on their podcast player.

On the other hand, if the expert is savvy about establishing their value, they will engage with you enthusiastically and authentically in a conversation about your shared area of interest. You will get to **know** them during this interaction, and if they treat you with courtesy and respect, you will begin to **relate** to them as well. If they demonstrate empathy for the challenges you're facing and share generously with advice based on their own experience, then you begin to **trust** them as well. Then when they mention, as your conversation is wrapping up, that they have a book coming out that covers some of the very topics you've discussed, you'll be excited about the opportunity to buy it, read it, and probably recommend it to others who could benefit from its information.

Be the podcast guest that brings that same attitude to your interviews. Maintain a focus on the know-relate-trust paradigm and on serving the audience rather than on making sales throughout the interview (and, in fact, throughout the entire process, from pitching through promotion of your host's podcast). If you serve your host and your audience, the sales will come naturally.

Offer a Value-first Invitation

Once you have provided value to the host and their audience through your conversation, you have laid the groundwork for inviting listeners to check out what else you have to offer related to your topic, and you've earned the right to extend this offer through your professionalism, preparedness and politeness. Hosts will normally give you an opportunity to highlight your offering at the end of the interview, and this is where a tasteful pitch is acceptable.

Make sure you understand your host's parameters for when and how you share this information. This is one of the many ways that listening to backlist episodes is helpful, but when in doubt, ask explicitly.

Mark is frequently approached by authors and their publicists who want to appear on *Stark Reflections on Writing and Publishing* in order to share something they want to sell. He turns down most of those pitches, not because he is averse to spotlighting services—he knows the value of the right service for the right author at the right time—but because he doesn't want the podcast to turn into an infomercial. He makes sure his guests understand that their conversation needs primarily to be a vehicle that delivers information, insights, and inspiration that Mark and his listeners can reflect on and learn from.

Matty often hosts guests on *The Indy Author Podcast* who have a writer-focused offering to pitch, but the guideline she provides to those guests is that a listener has to gain value from the podcast whether or not they use the guest's product or service. For example, when she hosted Damon Courtney of BookFunnel on the podcast, he shared valuable tips for author cross-promotion that listeners could act on even if they didn't use BookFunnel. Then, at the end of the interview, she invited him to provide a pitch for his product.

During your pitch, you might share the launch date of your upcoming book and mention the platforms where it will be available, or you might let the listeners know that you have products or services related to the topic of the discussion and where to find out more about them. If you craft your pitch around what *you have to offer them*—information, resources, support—rather than what they have to offer you—royalties or consulting fees—then you will have successfully carried an audience-focused message throughout your interview.

If you want to take your pitch to the next level, consider

personalizing an offer specifically for the podcast's listeners. This can be as simple as saying, "I have a special offer for listeners of the <podcast name> podcast," followed by a short, memorable URL that leads to a dedicated landing page. Creating a hidden page on your website—one that's not linked from your main navigation—is a straightforward way to do this. For example, you might set up *yourname.com/podcastname* and use it to offer a free resource, a discount code, or early access to a product or event.

This kind of personalization not only makes your pitch feel more tailored and generous, but it also allows you to track the effectiveness of your appearances. By monitoring traffic to the unique URL or downloads of your freebie, you can track how engaged each specific podcast audience was and which shows are bringing the most value. Over time, this builds a data set that can help you fine-tune future pitches, better understand your target audience, and even refine your offerings. Plus, a tailored offering creates a sense of exclusivity that can encourage more listeners to take action.

Remember that as a guest, your primary responsibility is to provide value to your host's audience. If you keep the audience's needs front and center—even when promoting your own work—your pitch will feel like a generous offer, not a sales tactic.

For Your Playbook

At the end of each section, we include questions for you to answer—capture your responses in the downloadable document available at theindyauthor.com/playbook. Doing so will encourage you to think through how the information in the book applies to your situation and how you will act on it. For this section ...

- What are two stories—one to engage and intrigue, one to educate and inspire—that you can share during a podcast interview to help establish your know-relate-trust relationship with listeners? Think about personal experiences, research insights, or challenges overcome that align with your topic and that show your relatability and credibility.
- How will you frame your closing pitch to highlight the value your book, product, or service offers to the audience, rather than what you hope to gain? Write a version of your closing that emphasizes helpfulness over hype.

DELIVERING YOUR INTERVIEW

In the section on "Building Rapport," we examined some of the strategic steps you can take to get and give the greatest value from your podcast appearances. In this section, we'll run through some of the more tactical tasks.

Final Preparations

It's the big day, and the time for your interview is fast approaching! What are the last steps you should take to demonstrate your preparedness and professionalism as a podcast guest?

- **Refresh your memory.** Even if you have only one primary topic for podcast interviews, you need to ensure that the information you're prepared to share matches the spin on that topic you proposed in your pitch. As you accumulate a portfolio of possible podcast topics, the importance of refreshing your memory becomes even more important. You don't want your first interaction with your host to be asking the question, "What are we talking about?"

- **Re-boot early.** Rebooting your computer an hour or so before the interview will ensure that you don't have apps running in the background that can degrade performance. Booting up the meeting platform software early will ensure that you won't be delayed by an unstoppable software re-install or update that could take several minutes.
- **Manage your space.** Make sure you have easy access to anything you might need during the conversation: a glass of water, your (very brief) notes, a book or other prop you might want to use. Mark likes to have pen and paper nearby so he can quickly jot down notes as ideas strike him during the conversation.
- **Run a test.** Run a test using the meeting platform to ensure that everything is in order; this avoids you having to make these adjustments when you sign onto the platform with your host. For example, if the interview will be conducted on Zoom, open a solo Zoom meeting (not the meeting on which the interview will be taking place) and check your set-up.
  - Check that the **mic, speakers, and camera** you'll be using are available.
  - **Lighting** is something you can't just set and forget; make sure it's set correctly for the time and environment of your interview.
  - Be sure that the **framing** of your video complies with the best practices we covered in the section on "Refining Your Virtual Presence." Make sure you're using that newscaster framing: the top of your head near the top of the frame, your body visible to about armpit level.

- ○ Check your **background**. Check for things like unintentionally open doors, uncurtained windows that might be casting more light into your studio space than you want, and anything untidy that might draw the viewer's eye.
- ○ Check your **appearance**. We're surprised by how many guests log in for their interview and then have to take some time to fix their hair or apply more makeup.

- **Reduce technical interruptions.** Set your computer (and your phone, if it will be nearby) to *do not disturb*. As an added precaution, we also recommend shutting down any apps that might interrupt your conversation, such as messaging apps or social media notifications, since these sometimes seem to consider themselves exempt from *do not disturb*.

- **Show up early.** If you're familiar with the meeting platform, sign on 10 minutes before the scheduled start time to get settled, run through your checklist, and address any tech issues. If you're *not* familiar with the platform, sign on 15 minutes early (assuming you've familiarized yourself with the platform before this). Recheck your audio and video settings, making sure you have the correct mic, speakers, and camera selected. Be prepared to begin the interview early if the host also arrives early.

- **Follow the host's lead.** Once you and the host have both signed on, different hosts will have different approaches. Some will dive right into the interview, probably with an eye to being respectful of your time. Some will spend some time chatting with you before starting to record in order to establish important touchpoints they want to ensure are covered and to build rapport. You should be prepared for either approach.

Pro tip: Before the interview begins, you might consider asking the host if you can record the interview (most virtual meeting platforms will allow participants to record a meeting with the host's authorization). Since this is not a standard guest request, this is something we would consider only if we had an established relationship with the host that would make them confident that we would use the recording in a responsible way —for example, not publishing any of the interview before the episode airs. We discuss how you might use this content in the section on "Creating Derivative Content."

Managing the Conversation

Here are a few reminders about how to act on the learnings you gained in the section on "Building Rapport."

Make it a conversation. You want the audience to feel like they're sitting at a kitchen table or at the local pub with you and the host for a relaxed, engaging chat. A conversation allows for spontaneity, curiosity, and give-and-take. Unlike a more rigid interaction, where the host asks pre-prepared questions and the guest delivers rehearsed answers, a conversation flows naturally, with room for tangents, laughter, and insight. When you and the host respond to each other in real time rather than sticking to a script, you'll uncover those "golden nuggets" of content that feel fresh and authentic—both to the host and to the audience.

Smile. Unless it seems inappropriate to your topic, a smile will help build rapport with the host and the audience; they will be able to hear a smile in your voice even if they are consuming the content on an audio-only platform.

Don't fake knowledge you don't have. If the host asks you a question and you don't know the answer, don't make one up. In fact, some of the most interesting conversations we've had as a guest on other podcasts is when we don't know the answer to a question, and we and the host try to figure it out together.

Feel comfortable with some silence. Taking a few seconds to think through your response to a question is fine—and better than filling the silence with filler words or verbal tics.

Dealing with the Outliers

Careful preparation and the few tips above will stand you in good stead for most interviews, but let's take a look at some exception cases.

For example, **what if the conversation seems to be straying too far from the agreed-upon topic?** Let's say you understood the topic of the interview to be a strategic discussion of how authors should decide whether to start a podcast and the strategy they should have in place if they decide to embark on one. However, the host starts steering the conversation toward the tech needed to produce a podcast. We recommend you make one attempt to steer the conversation back to the more strategic perspective, but if the host persists in the more tactical direction, go with it. You'll make a better impression on the audience if you engage enthusiastically in a topic the host is obviously enthusiastic about than if you continue to try to steer the conversation elsewhere. On top of that, the host understands their audience and their interests better than you do, so it's best to follow their lead. But be sure not to try to make something up if you don't know the answer. If, in this case, a tech question arises that you don't know the answer to, just say that that is not your area of expertise.

What if the tone turns argumentative? If possible, try to steer the conversation toward a topic you believe will be less emotional. Don't get into a verbal wrestling match with the host. Try to address the position they're taking or the question they're asking rather than the tone in which they might be expressing it. Remember that your ultimate audience is not your host, it's your host's listeners, so if the host is a jerk, don't be tempted to return bad behavior with bad behavior. That will just reflect badly on you.

For one livestreamed interview in which Mark was the guest, the host would ask Mark a detailed question that required a long and complex answer, then get up, walk around, and puff on a cigarette, seemingly completely uninterested in Mark's responses. It was distracting, disheartening, and rude. Mark maintained a professional demeanor by keeping in mind that he was ultimately there for the benefit of the audience, answering the questions as if the distracting and boorish behavior wasn't taking place. He continued the interview to the end, in fulfillment of his obligation, but after the interview was over, Mark informed his publicist of the host's unprofessional manner. Not only did Mark never want to be booked back on that show, but he also wanted to alert his publicist to the experience so he wouldn't pursue placements on that show for other clients.

We tell you this story not to alarm you—such situations are exceedingly rare—but to give you some tools to deal with these rare occurrences in order to give you the confidence that you are armed for any situation that might arise.

Have Your Closing and CTA Ready

As the interview wraps up, most hosts will give you the chance to tell the audience where to go to find more information about you and your work—be ready with a snappy response.

What should you include?

- A thank you to the host, with a comment about the experience (assuming it has been a positive one)
- A reference to your online "home"—usually your website—and perhaps a mention of one social media platform on which you're most active (audience members should be able to find all your social media profiles on your website)
- Your call to action / CTA

The CTA encapsulates what you want to gain from the appearance (for example, book sales, newsletter subscribers, social media followers, conference speaking engagements).

Keep your CTA brief! This not only keeps your appearance from devolving into an infomercial but also makes it easier for your audience to remember and therefore to act on the information you share.

For example, a closing for Matty might be:

Mark, thank you so much for inviting me to your podcast—I love talking with fellow podcasters about podcasting! If anyone would like to find out more about my fiction work, they can go to MattyDalrymple.com, and that's Matty with a Y. If they'd like to find out more about my nonfiction work, they can go to TheIndy Author.com, and that's Indy with a Y. I hope that they'll check out The Podcast Guest Playbook, *available in ebook, print, and audio on all major online retailers.*

A closing for Mark might be:

Thank you, Matty. It's always so wonderful getting a chance to chat with you. You can find out about me, my books, and links to my social media over at markleslie.ca. And if any of your listeners are interested in a free 20-minute consult with me to ask their own specific questions about the writing and publishing world, there's a form to book that time right there on my website.

Make sure you have the most important information at the end—e.g., in this example, if audience members do only one thing, Matty wants them to check out her book and Mark wants them to connect via his website.

What should you NOT include in your closing / CTA?

- DON'T include a reference to every social media platform you're on (and *definitely* don't include your handles on those sites).
- DON'T bother with the "double ewe double ewe double ewe dot" in front of your website name ... people don't need to type that in, and it's a wasted couple of seconds and 10 syllables.
- If you're pitching a book, DON'T overemphasize Amazon. Not everyone in the publishing industry has a positive perception of Amazon, and this is especially true among indie authors and bookstores. You don't want to introduce a sour note after all the work you've done to build a connection with your audience. If your book is exclusive to Amazon, mention that, but if it's wide—i.e., available beyond Amazon—don't say, "It's available on Amazon ... and all the other places you can find books." Instead, say, "It's available on all the major online retailers"; listeners will understand that this includes Amazon. And as Mark recommends in his book *An Author's Guide to Working with Libraries and Bookstores*, don't forget to let listeners know if they can find your book at their local library.

After the Wrap

After the *Live* or *Recording* light goes off, you'll normally still be on the meeting platform with the host, and this is a good time to get useful logistical information, such as when the episode might air and if the host will notify you when it goes live. You should also confirm your commitment to follow up on anything you owe the host, such as a link to a resource you mentioned in your conversation.

This is a great time to cement your connection to the host. Thank them for the opportunity. Mention specific aspects of the conversation that you particularly enjoyed. Let them know where you will be promoting the episode.

For Your Playbook

At the end of each section, we include questions for you to answer—capture your responses in the downloadable document available at theindyauthor.com/playbook. Doing so will encourage you to think through how the information in the book applies to your situation and how you will act on it. For this section ...

- What is on your checklist of things to do in the time leading up to the interview?
- How might you deal with an outlier situation—for example, a host who takes the conversation off-topic or who behaves unprofessionally?

AMPLIFYING YOUR APPEARANCE

We believe that one of the most common pitfalls podcast guests fall into is to believe their work is done when the interview is over. This not only undermines the benefits you can gain from community-building with the audience but dramatically reduces the benefits you can gain from connection-building with your host. The steps you take after the recording to amplify your appearance can pay back 80% of the dividends of a podcast appearance with 20% of the work—don't neglect this part of the process.

Immediately after the Interview

Here are a few steps you should take immediately after you sign off the interview platform.

- **Take a few moments to capture your thoughts.** These notes might include any specific items you committed to the host to follow up on as well as any actions not covered by your after-interview checklist. Also note any learnings you had from the conversation, such as a concept that you thought would be clear but that the host was obviously unsure about (and feed this into your planning for future interviews).

- **Send a thank you.** If you do this right away, you'll have readily to mind any comments you can use to personalize your thank you: *I especially appreciated your probing question about ...*

- **Record a teaser.** This idea came from Tom Schwab of Interview Valet: as soon as you sign off from the interview platform and while your conversation with the host is still fresh in your mind, record a quick video with a few sentences about the experience. This might be the major topics the episode covered, some special insight the conversation enabled, or a funny anecdote about the interview (as long as it doesn't paint the host in a bad light). Once the episode goes live, you can use this video, along with a link to the episode, as a more attention-getting and engaging way of highlighting the episode than a text or link-only post. (Even if you don't record this teaser immediately after a recording, you can do the same when you are able to watch or listen to the interview once it airs.)

When the Episode Airs

Most podcast hosts will let you know when your episode airs, but not always—check back periodically with that podcast in case you've missed it. Because Mark appears on so many podcasts, and he knows he won't always get a heads-up from the host or producer when an episode airs, he has set up an auto-mated Google Alert for his name and/or the specific topic or title of his most recent book.

When your interview airs, listen to it—if it's available in video, watch it—and take notes about the aspects of your delivery that ...

- ... you want to carry forward into future interviews.
- ... you want to avoid in future interviews.

For example, Matty's reviews of her performances as an interviewee remind her of the power of a sincere smile as well as the fact that a posture that might feel attentive can look grumpy or aggressive to a viewer. Once you've done that ...

Promote, promote, promote! This isn't just about the benefit you'll gain from your appearance—it's about showing respect and support for your host's platform.

It's surprisingly common for podcast guests to go to all the trouble of pitching a podcast (and all the work that entails) and prep for and conduct the interview but then not take full advan-tage of that opportunity. As a professional, don't be that guest! Otherwise, you undermine the value you, your host, and your audience can gain.

By promoting your episode—and, by extension, the podcast —actively, you establish yourself as a collaborative guest. Promo-tion goes beyond simply liking or resharing the host's posts. Add comments that amplify the value of the post and attract more attention. Include links to your appearance on your website and share the content on platforms the host might not typically reach.

Make sure your host knows you're spreading the word about your appearance. Tag them in your social media posts or send them a copy of your newsletter that highlights the event. If your promotional efforts are invisible to your host, you miss an opportunity to reinforce the professionalism and enthusiasm that can open doors to future opportunities.

In the week or so after the episode's airing, monitor all the platforms on which the host airs or promotes it so you're aware of any comments the listeners leave. This is not only great fodder for continuously improving your performance as a podcast guest, but you can further solidify your relationship with the listeners by responding to their comments—but only in a positive way! Hard as it may be, never respond to negative comments. (If you see anything especially egregious, let the host know—they can probably take down the comment if they agree it's inappropriate.)

If you mentioned another person or organization in a positive way (and beware of mentioning them in any way other than positive), be sure to flag them in any promotional posts on social media. That's not only a good way of encouraging others to share the content further but builds good karma.

Creating Derivative Content

If you have access to the interview audio or video files, and with the host's permission, you might create your own derivative content—for example, creating video clips, audiograms, text excerpts, stories, or reels. (If you don't have the tools or the knowledge to create these yourself, you can often find inexpensive support on marketplace platforms like Upwork or Fiverr.)

Always respect the host's brand and IP and, if in doubt about an idea you have for reuse, ask.

Sharing Evergreen Content

One of the beauties of podcasts is that your interviews will be available years after your appearances, even if the podcast itself is no longer active. That means that they can keep providing value for you and the listeners as long as the content is applicable.

Mark was a guest on a podcast back in 2006 called *The Writing Show with Paula B* talking about his novel *A Canadian Werewolf in New York*. Ten years later, Mark was at an in-person event selling books at an author table when someone approached his table, recognizing the title of one of his books because of his appearance on that episode ten years earlier.

If the content of an interview is evergreen, continue looking for opportunities to re-share it. Put a tickler note on your calendar to repost it periodically on social media or blog posts or to link to it in your newsletter. This will not only allow you to maximize the value you provided in the episode but also enable you to reach people who are not regular podcast listeners.

Consider collecting interviews with a common theme and scheduling periodic grouped re-promotions of the interviews. This strategy is most effective if each interview offers different information about the overall topic, which is another reason not to rely on a scripted stump speech for your podcast appearances.

The only cases in which this approach doesn't work is if your content is truly time-bound—for example, a review of a new piece of technology, or a commentary on a current event.

Inspiring a New Creation

There's a final way you can gain the greatest possible value from your podcast appearances, and it's one without which this book might never have come about.

When Matty first launched Pod Pro Author Coaching services, she wanted to provide a free resource for people who were looking for advice on diving into the world of podcast guesting. She created "The Indy Author's Guide to Podcast Guesting Checklist" based largely on the checklist she used for her own guest appearances.

But she wanted to provide something a little beefier that reflected what she had learned from her hundreds of episodes as the host of *The Indy Author Podcast* and her guest appearances on dozens more. Many of those episodes and appearances had addressed podcast guesting, and she began reviewing those to pick out the golden nuggets.

A few months later, she had created the skeleton of this book.

Shortly after that, Matty mentioned the book to Mark over lunch at an author conference, and considering our previous co-authoring experience and our mutual support for one another's podcasts, the idea of working on it together came up. A few email exchanges and video chats later, we began the collaborative process.

We've discussed ways you can use podcast guest appearances as a way to get word out about your book, but what if you have an area of expertise but do not yet have a book to back it up? Consider formalizing in book form the information you're sharing with your audience in your podcast appearances. This is not only a great source for content, but your interactions with your hosts and comments from your listeners can guide you in identifying concepts that might need fuller explanation or areas around which there is notable enthusiasm. All of this will enable you to expand your content from your appearances to the page even more effectively.

What If You Don't Want to Share It or Air It?

What if, despite all your careful preparation, a particular podcast appearance is one you wish you had never done? Maybe it's something fairly minor, like production quality. Maybe it's something more significant, like an unfortunate dynamic with the host. These situations are exceedingly rare, but it's important to have a plan for addressing them should they arise.

You Don't Want to Share it?

What if your concern is fairly minor, as with the poor production quality issue? The best solution in this case is just not to share it or otherwise publicize it. You may regret "wasting" the time and effort you've sunk into it but recognize that it's all part of the process. After all, it's not as if writers keep every single word they commit to paper. Some of those words end up on the cutting-room floor. "Killing your darlings" can refer not only to your words but also to your marketing and promotion efforts. Don't invest effort in an asset you feel will not deliver value to the community.

You Don't Want It to Air?

But what if your concern is more substantive? One example might be that on reflecting on the conversation the next day, you realize that you shared information you wish you hadn't.

For example, when Mark shares stories people have told him about first-hand ghostly encounters—as he does when promoting his paranormal nonfiction work—he normally takes care to protect the identity of those sources who want to remain anonymous. If he accidentally used the person's name or mentioned a detail that would make them identifiable, he might ask the host to cut out that question or perhaps bleep out one or two identifying words Mark used. Because Mark values and respects those who share their stories with him for his true ghost story books, not taking steps to address this issue would tarnish his journalistic reputation and violate his own personal moral code.

Matty experienced a similar situation from the host side when a guest discussed a topic during the interview that the guest later grew concerned might put sensitive information into the hands of bad players.

If this type of situation happens to you, do what Matty's guest did: contact the host as soon as possible, explain the reason for your concern, ask the host to remove the content in question (ideally a part of the interview, not the entire interview), and apologize for the inconvenience. But before you take this step, consider that you are asking the host to do what might be a significant amount of work to accommodate your request.

But what if the concern is based on something more personal, as with the example of an unpleasant dynamic with the host? What if you feel the content violates something important to you professionally or personally—for example, that listeners may take away a lesson that is the opposite of what you intended and believe in? What if you learn that the host has recently aligned themselves with a position you can't support? Contact them as soon as possible and request that they not air your episode. As necessary to support your request, share your reasons unemotionally and professionally. (If the episode has already aired, or if they refuse to comply with your request, then you may need to default to the "don't share it" approach; it's rarely useful to escalate such issues, which could just draw more attention to the situation.)

For Your Playbook

At the end of each section, we include questions for you to answer—capture your responses in the downloadable document available at theindyauthor.com/playbook. Doing so will encourage you to think through how the information in the book applies to your situation and how you will act on it. For this section ...

- What are the checklist items you will commit to do to amplify each podcast appearance to maximize the value to yourself, your host, and your audience?

MORE PERSPECTIVES, MORE OPPORTUNITIES

More Perspectives on Guesting

In *The Podcast Guest Playbook*, we've encapsulated everything we've learned about podcast guesting both from our own experiences and from the experiences of some of our podcast guests. If you'd like to hear more, we've provided below a list of some of our backlist episodes that focus on podcasts.

The Indy Author Podcast

Go to theindyauthor.com/episodes-all and search for *podcast* to find these and others—it's a topic Matty loves to discuss!

#220 - Podcasting Playbook: Navigating Guest Opportunities with Michelle Glogovac

#175 - Lessons Learned as an Author Podcaster and YouTuber with M.K. Williams and Matty Dalrymple

#137 - Using Podcasts to Support Your Book Launch with Michelle Glogovac

#51 - Podcasting as Content Marketing with Jerri Williams

#21 - Building Communities with Podcasts with J. Thorn

Stark Reflections on Writing and Publishing

Go to https://starkreflections.ca to find these episodes.

#393 – Book Adjacent Strategies with Jodi Swannel (Jody talks about becoming a radio host – adjacent to podcast hosting)

#383 – From Page to Platform: How to Succeed as an Author Speaker with Matty Dalrymple and M.L. Ronn

#216 – Podcasting for Authors with Matty Dalrymple

#183 – Baring it All with Jenn Taylor, the Naked Podcaster

#19 – Cashing in on Creativity with Bruce Outridge

Radio & Television Interviews

The Podcast Guest Playbook focuses specifically on podcast appearances, but many of the same best practices apply to radio and television interviews. We provide some additional tips specific to those formats here.

As with podcasts, radio and television interviews are sometimes pre-recorded and sometimes air live, and they are often conducted on a virtual platform. However, interviews with *local* radio and television outlets are sometimes conducted in person at the station. Since we don't explore in-person interviews in much depth earlier in the book, here are a few tips to keep in mind for these situations:

- **Scout the location.** Make sure you know where you're going for the interview, either by doing a drive-by in advance or via Google Maps and Street View. Try to determine where you'll park and how you'll access the building. You don't want to be flustered by the inability to find the entrance the day of the interview.
- **Scout out the show**. As with podcasts, you'll want to listen to or watch previous segments that are similar to the one you'll be interviewed for, but this

is especially important for in-person television appearances. You can glean information about the seating arrangement, camera placement, and background.

- **Arrive early.** To avoid the added stress of concern about your schedule, allow plenty of time to get to the interview locations. Also make sure you understand the timing of the full event—you might be scheduled to air a live segment at noon, but the station might need you there early for makeup, mic fitting, or sound checks. (And speaking of makeup, television stations will sometimes have a makeup artist to apply makeup to reduce the appearance of perspiration or shininess, but although they apply it, they rarely remove it. If you're not headed home right after your interview, pack a makeup remover towelette for this purpose.)

- **But not TOO early.** Television and radio stations often have limited space, and if you arrive far in advance of the requested time, the station might not be able to accommodate you right away in their guest intake process or have room for you in their green room or other guest accommodations. Find a nearby coffee shop to pass the time until your scheduled arrival time or do some deep breathing exercises in your car.

Podcasting Beyond Guesting

You might find yourself so intrigued by the possibilities offered by podcasting that you find yourself considering becoming a podcast host yourself. We have you covered! In *The Indy Author's Guide to Podcasting for Authors*, Matty shares her learnings from her years hosting and producing *The Indy Author Podcast*. Tapping into nautical metaphors to explore the stages of creating a podcast, *Podcasting for Authors* will guide you through determining your destination, preparing for your voyage, and setting sail. Matty discusses the benefits podcasting offers to authors specifically, and the specific challenges authors might need to overcome to succeed in this medium. Questions posed at the end of each chapter prompt insights to be captured in your own Captain's Log, enabling you to note progress, acknowledge mistakes, and celebrate successes on your voyage.

Hosting a podcast can be a significant investment of time and energy, and *Podcasting for Authors* allows readers to understand what it takes to produce a podcast before taking the plunge. But the decision doesn't have to be either/or—many podcasters are creating limited series podcasts, perhaps in support of a particular event, like a book launch, or based on a time-bound topic, like techniques for getting your writing done during the holidays. This is a great way to dip your toe in the podcasting waters and find out if the life of a podcast host is for you!

Speaking Beyond Guesting

If you're planning your podcast appearances as part of a larger career as an author speaker, check out the book Matty coauthored with M.L. Ronn, *From Page to Platform: How to Succeed as an Author Speaker*. Establishing yourself as a successful speaker is both an art and a science. Where do you start? *From Page to Platform* is your essential blueprint to making that leap. This comprehensive guide will help you land your first speaking engagements, deliver captivating presentations, and build a respected brand as a speaker.

You'll learn how to ...

- Define your speaking goals and craft your unique message.
- Connect deeply with your audience, in-person or virtually.
- Land your first paid speaking engagement.
- Discover the secrets to creating impactful slides.
- Impress organizers and ensure you're always in demand.

Whether you're an experienced author or just starting out, *From Page to Platform* offers insightful strategies, practical steps, and the inspiration you need to share your voice with the world from the stage.

Building Your Author Brand

And if you're interested in strategies related to creating and maintaining an effective author brand—of which being a guest on podcasts and other media is definitely a part—check out Mark's book *A Writer's Guide to Branding for Success: Strategies, Ideas, and Tactics for Leveraging Your Most Valuable Author IP Asset.* This book explores techniques that not only international brands but also successful authors have employed to engage, compel, and deliver the right promise to the right readers (and listeners) at the right time, and help you ask the right questions to examine your author brand and set the stage for refining and re-imagining your brand. Whether you know it or not, you already have an author brand. But it's time to take control of it and allow it to work for you.

For Your Playbook

At the end of each section, we include questions for you to answer—capture your responses in the downloadable document available at theindyauthor.com/playbook. Doing so will encourage you to think through how the information in the book applies to your situation and how you will act on it. For this section ...

- Do any of the opportunities beyond podcast guesting—radio and television interviews, podcast hosting, speaking beyond podcasting, or building your author brand—sound appealing to you?

CONCLUSION

There is always more to discover as a podcast guest. Even after hundreds of appearances, we still find that each interview teaches us something new—whether it's finding additional ways to capitalize on the content that we and our hosts create, how to pivot smoothly when a question takes us by surprise, or the best way to transform an awkward silence into an unforgettable beat. Guesting wisdom means recognizing which shows align best with your message, pitching them with confidence, and showing up prepared to delight the listeners. It means ensuring that every interaction brings value to yourself, your host, and your audience. It means drawing a steady stream of curious listeners to your work and forging relationships that outlast any single episode. Ultimately, it's having such a firm grasp of the process that you anticipate a host's needs before they voice them and answer audience questions before they're asked.

That level of mastery delivers all the professional and personal rewards of being a true, long-term collaborator in the podcasting sphere—and, as you've probably noticed, it looks a lot like the professionalism you cultivate as a creator.

We hope the guidance in *The Podcast Guest Playbook* helps

you turn conversations into lasting connections and thriving community. Drop us a line and let us know how your journey is going!

Matty@MattyDalrymple.com
Mark@MarkLeslie.ca

ACKNOWLEDGMENTS

Huge thanks to ...

Jerri Williams, host of the FBI Retired Case Files Review podcast, for sharing her expertise on using podcasts for content marketing.

Michelle Glogovac of The MLG Collective and author of *How to Get on Podcasts*, for sharing her learnings as both a host and a guest.

Matty's special guests on Episode 220 of *The Indy Author Podcast*, "Podcasting Playbook: Navigating Guest Opportunities" and beyond—Melissa Addey, Emma Dhesi, Michael La Ronn, Diane Vallere, Jerri Williams, and Frank Zafiro—for sharing their tips for excelling once you land the guest appearance.

Tom Schwab of Interview Valet for permission to use quotes from and references to his work.

Mary Dalrymple, for once again lending us her eagle proofreading eye.

And finally, Matty and Mark would like to thank all of the guests who have honored them by appearing on *The Indy Author Podcast* and *Stark Reflections on Writing and Publishing* over the years.

ABOUT THE AUTHORS

Matty Dalrymple educates and advocates for writers as The Indy Author. She is the host and producer of hundreds of episodes of *The Indy Author Podcast* and has spoken on topics related to writing and publishing at events such as the Writer's Digest annual conference, the Alliance of Independent Authors' SelfPubCon, Author Nation, Authors Guild webinars, International Thriller Writers' CraftFest, and many more. She writes nonfiction books for writers, and her articles have appeared in *Writer's Digest* magazine, *Indie Author Magazine*, and ALLi's *The Indie Author* magazine. She serves as ALLi's Campaigns Manager. Learn more at https://www.theindyauthor.com/

Matty is also the author of the Lizzy Ballard Thrillers, beginning with *ROCK PAPER SCISSORS*; the Ann Kinnear Suspense Novels, beginning with *THE SENSE OF DEATH*; and the Ann Kinnear Suspense Shorts. She is a member of International Thriller Writers and Sisters in Crime. Learn more at https://www.mattydalrymple.com/

Mark Leslie Lefebvre has been writing since 1984 and has worked in the book industry since 1992. A long-time advocate for digital publishing and helping authors understand the business of writing and publishing, Mark has been podcasting on and off since 2006, been a guest on hundreds of podcasts and radio programs, and has released weekly episodes of his Stark Reflections on Writing and Publishing podcast since January 2018.

Mark's roles in the book industry have included bookstore manager, President of the Canadian Booksellers Association, Director of Self-Publishing & Author Relations at Rakuten Kobo (where he created and launched Kobo Writing Life), Director of Business Development for Draft2Digital, Professional Advisor for Sheridan College's Honors Degree in Creative Writing and Publishing, board member for BookNet Canada, Library and Bookstore Advisor for ALLi, an esteemed judge for Writers of the Future, and founding board member for Superstars Writing Seminars and Wide for the Win.

Under the name Mark Leslie, he is the author of numerous horror and thriller novels, including his *Canadian Werewolf* novels, and the editor of speculative anthologies. Under his full name he has written and co-authored more than a half dozen books for writers. Find out more at www.markleslie.ca.

ALSO BY MATTY DALRYMPLE

More Than a Jest

Our Dancing Days

Sea of Troubles

Stage of Fools

These Hot Days

Wondering Eyes

Write in Water

Non-Fiction

Taking the Short Tack: Creating Income and Connecting with Readers Using Short Fiction with Mark Leslie Lefebvre

The Indy Author's Guide to Podcasting for Authors: Creating Connections, Community, and Income

From Page to Platform: How to Succeed as an Author Speaker with M.L. Ronn

Collaborate to Create: A Guide to Coauthoring Nonfiction with M.L. Ronn

The Podcast Guest Playbook: Turning Conversations into Connections and Community with Mark Leslie Lefebvre

Published by William Kingsfield Publishers

Cover design by Matty Dalrymple

Cover image by kittyfly via Deposit Photos

ISBN-13: 978-1-959882-22-0 (Ebook)

ISBN-13: 978-1-959882-24-4 (Paperback)